One Mile to Make a Difference

Seven miles to change direction!

SIMEON STURNEY

Sarah
GRACE
PUBLISHING

They asked each other, 'Were not our hearts burning within us while he talked with us on the road and opened the Scriptures to us?' They got up and returned at once to Jerusalem.'
(Luke 24:32-33)

I dedicate this book to my family who have journeyed with me through many 'ups' and several 'downs' over the years; and to the women I journey alongside who have also had their fair and unfair share of many 'downs' and not enough 'ups' as yet. Together we are stronger!

What Others Are Saying

Read this book – it will open your eyes.

Fiona, former
Her Majesty's Prison resident

Having worked for several years with women in custody, I have observed the effect it has on them. They come in through the gate in fear of the unknown. Sadly, as they leave through the gate, for some there is even greater fear of the known. That short walk from the prison to the station exposes their vulnerability to whomever or whatever can lure them back to a lifestyle that can only lead them back down a slippery path. In reading this book you will see cameos of an important ministry carried out by a man of God. A practical act, day by day, of Christian kindness, in a world that could not care less – showing there is a God who could not care more.

Marian Henderson,
Salvation Army Chaplain

One Mile to Make a Difference is an amazing read: simple, profound, enlightening and practical. Simeon takes us on a journey few of us have made. Every page rings with authenticity and we are invited to walk in his shoes as he accompanies prisoners facing life outside. I am thrilled that Simeon has given us this insight into his life as a prison chaplain and his through-the-gate mission. It is a call to involvement – prepare to be illuminated and inspired.

Nigel Tween, Director:
Elim Chaplain Association –
elim.org.uk/chaplains

Simeon, I am thrilled to be associated with this book. By all standards your rich experience will have great impact on future generations of prison chaplains in no uncertain terms. We appreciate your selflessness and sacrifice for prisoners as they walk out of the gates in a world of uncertainty. Grateful for sharing your life experiences with the world and enhanced the fight against recidivism.

Revd Canon Selwyn S.A. Okai,
Chief Superintendent of Prisons, Regional
Chaplain Accra, Ghana

Contents

Foreword

'Make them pay', 'No justice', 'Longer sentences', 'Failed system'. These are some of the headlines that we see sensationalised by the press. The phrases 'Serial killer', 'Terrorist', 'Organised Crime', 'Gangs' are exactly the headlines some people want to hear so then they can say that we knew the person in the spotlight was a 'bad un' and definitely guilty! 'They should lock them up and throw away the key!' My goodness, I have heard that phrase so many times and probably uttered it myself! I used to be one of the self-righteous, so secure in the knowledge that my life was going to be perfect. That is until I found myself in prison a few years ago.

Where did it go so wrong? What does it take for someone to commit a crime? What were the choices that led to that particular pathway? Nature verses Nurture? I was bought up in a very strict Church of England household. This involved church every Sunday, my father was a church warden and both my parents were very involved in the church community and, by association, so were my sister and I. I managed, through the ups and downs of life, to keep my faith but the disillusion with organised religion culminated at my lowest point when some Christians in my life disowned me – but that is a whole other story! Life is messy, seriously messy! So at that horrific point in my life where I had sinned so terribly I genuinely believed that I did not deserve to live and I still struggle with these demons all these years later. So when Simeon approached me saying that he had written a book and would I write the foreword, I had that moment of 'Oh my goodness!' It took a while for me to start reading, in the knowledge that it would be bringing back memories that are difficult for me.

I had the pleasure of meeting Simeon at the lowest point in my life and will never forget that first meeting! I was a broken and shattered husk of a person and there in prison I met Simeon, this bubbly, positive, bundle of energy. His opening words being, 'Hi, I'm Simeon,' and then he just sat and listened – really listened. Simeon is just 'one of the good ones', it's hard to explain. Maybe 'filled with the Holy Spirit' is a better description? He will be astounded by my description of him as I don't think he realised the good effect he has on people by just being himself. Whatever it is, he has the ability to really connect with a person with no agenda or preaching involved and genuinely cares, ever so often to the detriment of himself! With the help of Simeon, other amazing members of staff and the girls, I found my faith and I found myself. I would love to say that I found a path to forgive myself but that's still a work in progress.

It would be great if after my release I could confirm that society welcomed me back with loving and supportive arms but that is just not the case. There is a perception that once you are released your life goes on and I am here to attest that, unfortunately, this just does not happen. People can be so disparaging and condemning of repeat offenders but in most cases, what are their options? How would you fare if you had no money and your bank accounts were frozen; your house was up for sale so you needed to find somewhere to live but you have no bank account and no regular income; you can't get insurance except from specialist insurers who charge a loaded premium; and there is no help available from charities as you are too qualified? Also, you can't get a job where a Disclosure and Baring Service (DBS) check is done – believe me, I've tried! People love to hear your story but never offer you the job! In addition to all this you are still struggling with your mental health; you have lost the bulk of your 'friends' and EVERYONE knows what you have done! Then you go through a divorce so you have no husband and your family disowns you. It's not just the time inside prison that you have to contend with, it is the time before trial and also the licence period upon release and the time on your DBS record. And just to top it all off, you keep punishing yourself and struggle to let yourself move on. All of this was my experience and is the experience of many other people that Simeon writes about in this book.

I was so lucky to have the support of my true friends, Simeon and a house to go back to, even if it was only for a temporary time. I love them so much for all the support and unconditional love they gave me. Read this book – it will open your eyes.

Fiona
Former resident of Her Majesty's Prison
October 2019

Introduction
The Journey of a Lifetime

Golden beaches and far-flung exotic destinations which take months if not years of planning and saving for are often what we think of when we ponder the 'journey of a lifetime'. Yet some significant and equally memorable journeys can be a lot closer to home and shorter in length. The journey down the wedding aisle as a single person precedes the return journey as a married couple and perhaps exciting new challenges, or the journey to the hospital in labour with a baby just about to be born – fresh starts and new beginnings can be exciting times and yet daunting as well. Terrifying can be the journey to a funeral of a family member or friend, leaving devastation in its wake. Every day there are hundreds of people embarking on a 'journey of a lifetime'. This number also includes people beginning new careers, unaware of where it may take them and how long that journey will go on for, perhaps a lifetime!

This is a story of three particular journeys. It begins with a little of my own story, a journey from managing and overcoming disability, to the ministry I have today – supporting people the moment they come out of prison. I also look in detail at the journey those recently released from prison make and link it with the journey the two followers of Jesus made on the road to Emmaus. This book looks at Jesus' example of journeying with people who appear to be going in the wrong direction as seen in the Emmaus Road passage; and through the questions at the end of every chapter it challenges us to look at how we can support those around us who also appear to be heading in the wrong direction, as well as how we can get the support we need when we, too, walk on the wrong path.

Some journeys on the surface don't appear to be too difficult or significant, but look a little deeper and take time to retrace the steps and sometimes a surprise or two are revealed. When I reflect upon the journey I have made I am amazed at God's grace and mercy, and how he was at my side even when I thought I was a failure. I can look back and see the plan he had for me and see the plans he has for some of those I journey with. I guess those two people walking to Emmaus never thought the day would end the way it did; everyone can be surprised.

This book gives a little background to the work I do as a through-the-gate chaplain and how some of the women may have found themselves behind bars; followed by a few observations from behind the scenes as they wait to be released, travel on foot past a local shop and a couple of churches, and finish up at the railway station. I conclude the book by looking at how people can get involved in supporting those who have been recently released from prison.

The 'critical hour'

One Mile to Make a Difference is not only the story of journeys made but also about the time they take. My story is of a lifetime. The story of the two on the road to Emmaus would have been over a period of several hours. The journey the women take from the holding cell in the prison to the town's train station can take around an hour. In relation to the release process, this is often called the 'critical hour'. In other areas of work such as the Health Service and emergency care, the first hour following trauma is often referred to as the 'golden hour'. This period is critical to whatever recovery is possible. The first hour, or in my experience the first mile, is also critical to how the woman is going to fare for the rest of the day and even for her entire resettlement back into the community. As you read the book you will understand how significant the first hour or first mile is to the whole rehabilitation process. That first hour can fly past or drag, the whole process of leaving the area seemingly taking hours, whereas in reality women can be on the train within an hour of leaving their cell. The pace of this book is set by pace of the journey the women take as they make their way from inside the establishment to the train station; some rush it while others dawdle.

Confidentiality

I share various anecdotes regarding the women I journey alongside. However, I have changed all their names. In fact, I have changed all the names in the book except those in the acknowledgements – and even then I have only put their first names. I had at one point called the women 'Ms A, Ms B, Ms C', etc. But I found this to be very impersonal. I told a woman recently that I was writing a book about what I do. She asked me if she was in it. I told her she wasn't but, as I reflected, I noted that her name was mentioned in the book, although the anecdote was about someone completely different. Currently we have a through put of approximately four thousand women each year, so although I've changed the names and in some cases the details of the actual event to uphold confidentiality, some people may still think a particular anecdote is about them. However, the route we take is the same, passing the same buildings and arriving at the same railway station; a significant number swear and pop into the local shop, so there is a lot of overlapping. What I have found surprising is how many women have asked me to include them in the book when I mentioned I was writing it, so many want their story to be told.

Be encouraged

I hope the narrative will encourage you to journey with those who appear to be taking the wrong pathway. If you are already some way along that specific journey with someone close to you then I hope this book will encourage you to keep going. If your own journey is taking you in a direction you never dreamt it would and is really hard right now, keep alert because God might just send someone to journey alongside you for a while, but you may not even be aware of God's involvement until the person has moved on. Jesus said, 'And surely I am with you always, to the very end of the age' (Matthew 28:20).

Chapter 1
Behind The Scenes

My journey

'Sorry, lad, you're too thick.' They may not have been the exact words the Army chaplain used, but that is what I took away from our brief conversation. I had joined the Royal Corps of Signals as a Junior Signalman when I was sixteen years old and was stationed over two hundred and fifty miles away from home for my basic six-months training. Yet after only two and a half months I knew this was not the career I wanted, even though I had gone through an extensive selection process which had taken many months including various tests, interviews and a weekend away at an Army camp in Didcot, Oxfordshire. I had come to the conclusion that there was only one job in the Army I wanted to do and that was to be a chaplain or, as called in the military, padre. I had recently firmed up my Christian faith by making a private vow to follow Jesus wherever he took me. However, I had already started the journey of becoming a soldier so I continued along this path. I don't remember all of the conversation with the padre but to this day I still remember how deflated I felt. Of course he was right, in that I wasn't academic enough for such a role. Almost immediately an air of resignation hovered over me because this was not the first time my academic ability was highlighted as being below the standard required and it wasn't going to the last time either.

For years I had struggled at school work and for one and a half years in the late 1960s I had been seconded to a special education needs project in Essex; it was called the Opportunity Class. We were a group of junior school children around the ages of seven to eleven, who had been assessed as having reading and writing difficulties. We had been gathered together from all over the county and met as a full-time special needs class in a mainstream school, akin to a special needs school within a school. Alongside attending this project I also had a one-to-one special needs session once a week away from the school. In 1970 we moved as a family from Essex to west London where there was no such project. Fairly soon after arriving at my new school I began attending extra sessions during school time for my reading skills, which were still poor. These sessions finished when I was eleven years old and resumed for my last year of my secondary schooling when I was fifteen.

Structured expectations

I remember having painful conversations throughout my schooling with my mother who began to structure my expectations and told me that I was unlikely to get a good job – in fact she was very specific and said my job would be to stack shelves in a shop. She also added that I wouldn't get married as no girl would want to marry someone with a poorly paid job. So joining the Army was a relief to me as this meant I had a job with prospects lined up regardless of what grades I got in my exams. Needless to say my grades were not good at all.

Whilst my mother's comments weren't meant to be harsh, they weren't particularly encouraging or helpful; honesty doesn't always help. However, she had been incredibly helpful in teaching me to read. I remember her sitting down with me every day listening as I struggled with some very basic books. She often displayed great patience with those who were struggling and had difficulties, but not so patient if all was well in life. We often had visitors to the house who had various issues and disabilities; it must have been at these times I saw the positive impact of journeying with people who are in the margins of society – in that sphere my mother was a great role model and I learnt a lot from her. Sadly, Mum didn't always cope well with the stresses of life and on several occasions, even when I accidentally messed up, I got a whack or two.

Working it out

When I came out of the Army I worked for a short while in a hotel as a general porter. At this time I also had a careers assessment which identified me as being suitable for work in the care sector, residential care in particular. Whilst I didn't have the required grades, I was still accepted on an introductory social care course at a local college; this was because I was a male and they had very few young men apply. During my time at college I was at last formally assessed as having dyslexia – a specific learning disability. I never tire of reading the educational psychologist's report on me: 'He is of rather above average intelligence but handicapped in harnessing this to academic tasks by a specific learning disability or dyslexia probably associated with the following features . . .' (he goes on to list nine features). That report, written over forty years ago, helped change my life; there was now a clearly defined reason for my academic struggles which really eased my mind.

I left college having successfully completed the course and began a career in social care which spanned nearly twenty-five years. Eventually I found myself being made redundant and forced to apply for a job in an unrelated field of work. Once again, although not having the required grades or qualification, a theme throughout my years of employment, I was appointed as a Probation Service Officer in a soon-to-be-opened women's prison. Still being on good terms with God, I told him that I would like to do this for no more than three years. Over six years later I was still there! Feeling the urge to do something in which I could share my Christian faith more overtly, I applied for and was appointed to the role of Community Chaplaincy Project Manager within the same prison. Six months later I was appointed as the Chaplaincy Team Manager and two years later I was commissioned as a prison chaplain, only thirty-six years after I had first wanted to become a chaplain – what a journey!

For years I had preached in various churches and had taken on junior leadership roles. I approached my denomination – Elim Pentecostal Church – and they enabled me to fulfil this ambition. This appointment also made me the prison's Managing Chaplain, incidentally a position I was still not academically qualified for. I believe I was Elim's first Managing Chaplain of a prison, certainly of a women's prison. After holding the post of Chaplaincy Manager / Managing Chaplain for five years in total, I felt God call me to step out from that role and trust him for a new adventure. Although I had left my paid role I was still kept on as a volunteer chaplain and then as a paid cover chaplain, eventually being brought back on staff and contracted as a part-time through-the-gate chaplain, an uncommon job title and one I will explain in detail later, as well as the role of a prison chaplain.

So far

It has been an amazing journey for me so far. But that's the point – so far! It's not finished yet; although it has also been a long journey I'm sure there is more to come. I was born to Missionary parents on a little island in the South Pacific – Aitutaki (pronounced eye-tu-taki), Cook Islands. There were complications at birth and I nearly died but after prayer and the emergency interventions of the local doctor, as well as 'welding oxygen', my life was saved. The lack of oxygen at birth may have contributed to brain damage and the subsequent learning disability that has journeyed with me all my life. The miraculous account of my birth and the support from Dr Snowball and others at the time is quite another story. There are several stories I'd like to tell you, some less factual including one about a six-legged blue hobbling and another story about a one-legged robin called 'John' (but I can't because his name isn't 'John'). I value whimsy and enjoy a vivid imagination and a wacky sense of humour. Humour is needed at times as it brings a balance and often lightness to dark situations and I've experienced a few of those throughout my life.

After full-time education I found employment, got married, had two wonderful children and eventually owned my own day service for people with learning disabilities. My mother's predictions did not come true – praise God! I know she was also pleased she got that one wrong. Life hasn't always been easy for me and some people have made judgements concerning me without the facts. They have presumed my education was 'top notch', attending a good university or theological college. And the truth is – it was 'top notch' for me because it was what God wanted for me, but that hasn't included going to university or obtaining a degree – yet. My journey has led me to the here and now, to walking with people who know what broken feels like, a feeling I have also known. I have been equipped to understand just a little of how it may feel for those I have the honour to walk alongside.

Having travelled on this crazy working life journey for over forty years from Junior Signalman to that of Managing Chaplain of a women's prison, via the social care sector and without the relevant qualifications for many of the posts I've held, there are times I just stop and marvel at how God has not only led and guided me but how he has helped me overcome my disability and the unhelpful labels such as 'thick' or 'stupid' and the feeling of failure; to reach a position where I can now journey with those who are also used to being labelled as 'failures', 'thick' and 'stupid'. I enjoy travelling with people through the ups and downs of life and feel privileged to journey with those who often feel they are at their lowest point: a life in prison. Perhaps it is of no surprise that as a preacher, one of my favourite stories in the Bible is centred on the two followers of Jesus on the road to Emmaus found in Luke's gospel. In my current role I walk with the women being released from prison as they make their way to the local train station. This can be a journey filled with anxiety, confusion and sometimes disappointment, just as it was for those followers of Jesus as they left Jerusalem and headed towards Emmaus.

A central theme of this book is the story of what it can be like for some women as they leave prison and start out on their journey back into the community, with all of their hopes and fears. As I lead you along the road the women take to the station, I will also pause to reflect on the journey Jesus' followers took as they escaped Jerusalem, feeling lost, saddened and confused. Their story ends with them realising that Jesus had journeyed with them whilst they were at their lowest point and how, realising this, they were encouraged to re-join their friends with a new-found passion and hope. I believe Christians are encouraged to follow Jesus' lead and journey with those people who need extra support, many of whom see themselves in the margins of society, including some who have come out of prison. It is my hope that you may be prompted to pray for such people and perhaps get involved with supporting those who have experienced prison life.

Welcome to prison

The road towards prison that many women take is often a circuitous route, taking many turns and venturing into a variety of physical and emotional states before finally landing at a destination they never thought they would locate or ever wanted to arrive at. Their journey out of prison can be equally as challenging for them, sometimes even more so. On their pathway to prison, many women have experienced abuse of some form – physical, emotional, sexual or financial – perpetrated by people with significant influence, power and control over them, very often men.

Some women can land in prison feeling exhausted from their journey, both physically and mentally. As there are fewer female prisoners and therefore fewer women's prisons, women can be transported on long journeys from the court where they are sentenced, to a prison often geographically many miles away from where they live. They can feel emotionally 'burnt out' and in their lowest state of mind. For some women all hope appears to have been lost, every desperate attempt to stave off what now has become their reality and drained every ounce of their resolve to fight, has dissipated into the gloom that hovers over their situation.

Here, some women can feel like they have lost everything and the future is bleak. These emotions are not unique to women prisoners – men sentenced to prison can also share these thoughts. However, there is often another level of emotional grief placed upon women and that comes in the form of 'guilt'. Sometimes this is put on them by family, friends or even society, who can all think they should have taken their responsibilities towards their family more seriously and not engaged in the process that has now separated them from those they are supposed to be caring for. And when the guilt doesn't come from outside sources, it can be generated from within, by the woman herself, believing she has let people down.

So the woman finds herself in prison, living with the thoughts that she is now separated from those who have cared for her and those she should be caring for. She can tell herself she has failed in so many ways: by committing the offence or offences that have finally driven her to prison; failed to be the daughter, sister, wife and mother she should have been; and failed herself and her dreams.

There is a saying in prison that is true in life: 'It is what you make it.' There are opportunities in prison for women and men to learn different skills, address their offending behaviour and set new goals for their future. Assessments are carried out and interviews should take place to help support the prisoner to challenge their own thinking and restore hope.

However, for those men and in particular those women who not only previously have been told that they are 'useless' and will never achieve anything, that no one wants them anymore; they may be labelled 'scum' or 'slag', and can still hear this while in prison. They hear this from their family, friends and the wider society through visits, on the phone, letters or in the press. What hope have they got of taking advantage of what is on offer while they are in prison: 'Why bother as I'm scum anyway and nobody wants to know me?' 'What's the point of trying anymore?' Another familiar view often shared by someone who has lost everything and knows that when they return to the community there will be no one there for them other than some official telling them what they already know: 'Don't get into any more trouble – or else.' Motivation in and out of prison can disappear very quickly, especially if ties are lost with the outside.

So often how a woman copes with her release from prison is related to how she entered the prison. If, when she was convicted and sentenced, she still had the support of some family members, support from her friends or social networks and knows they would be there for her during her imprisonment and subsequent return to the community, she can begin this next leg of her journey with some hope, albeit temporarily muted – given the circumstance – the guilt assuaged to some degree.

When a woman is completely saturated with guilt, hopelessness, loneliness and despair, then her own plans for her release are already under serious threat. If when she stares out of her prison cell window and sees nothing but 'darkness', then all she is expecting to see when she is released is that same 'darkness'.

Emotional gloom is one of the most significant challenges a woman may face at the point of her release. She may also come across people who were once close to her but now want to keep a cold, silent distance. The stigma attached to women leaving prison can be viewed a little differently to that applied to men. Women can easily be viewed as 'having failed' whereas for some men it is more focused on 'having been caught'. Men and women who come out of prison can face prejudice and limitations on how they can integrate back into community. But women can also face ongoing abuse, especially from scorned family and friends.

For many women at the point of their release, while they wait for the main gate to open, they do not know who is really going to be there for them, physically and emotionally. Who is going to be there for their journey with no strings attached, no extra guilt trips added, no throwing up the past at every opportunity? Some women don't even know where they are going to sleep that night or where their next meal is coming from. Some leave in such a rush that they haven't had any breakfast before they leave and may not eat for the rest of the day. Many don't know if they will ever taste 'success' or be reunited with their children, or be welcomed at family events in the future. There are women who don't know if they will have secure employment ever again, safe accommodation and live in peace not fear; being truly free from past mistakes, hang-ups and in some cases addictions.

The challenge for many women as they leave prison is whether they will fare any better than before they went in. If they went in 'broken', then what does 'mended' look like, how long does it take and what is the process? Then come the thoughts again – 'Will I ever be okay? Is there anyone who can help me?'

The chaplain

The primary role of a chaplain is two-fold. A chaplain is someone who represents a particular faith or belief system and is in post to enable those of the same faith to practise their religion according to its teachings and beliefs. The chaplain also has a duty of care towards all the people in the prison, prisoners and staff; those of faith and of no faith. There are clear guidelines set out by Her Majesty's Prison and Probation Services as to how chaplaincy teams must operate within the prison.

Each chaplain appointed is endorsed by the faith group they represent and by Prison Chaplaincy Headquarters. Almost all prisons will have on staff chaplains from the Christian community, including people from the Church of England, the Roman Catholic Church and what is called the Free Church – they may be Methodist, Baptist, Pentecostal, Evangelical or from an independent church. Every prison is likely to have representatives from the Islamic community as well as from various other faiths. During my time as Managing Chaplain we had faith leaders in our team representing Christianity, Islam, Hinduism, Sikhism, Judaism, Buddhism, Paganism, Jehovah's Witnesses as well as someone from the Latter-day Saints. Most of these were part time. We had so many because we had prisoners of all these faiths. They all led study classes in addition to corporate worship and offered pastoral support.

Alongside their faith-related duty, chaplains are expected to carry out 'statutory duties'. Every day of the year, chaplaincy teams must visit prisoners in the establishment's healthcare wing, if they have one, as well as people in the Separation and Care Unit – the prison within the prison. They are also duty bound to interview every new prisoner, ideally within twenty-four hours of their arrival. These visits are primarily focused on welfare and support. Another significant aspect of the welfare support they give is in the area of bereavement and serious illness. If a prisoner receives bad news concerning someone close to them then it is the role of the chaplain to offer comfort and clarity. Sometimes it is the chaplain who is bringing the sad news. Before they do this they have to check with authorities outside of the prison that the information they have is correct; this may involve telephoning a hospital or a funeral director. On occasions, the prisoner may receive the information through a letter or when they make a phone call to a relative or friend. If a close family member has died then an application to attend their funeral may be made by the prisoner. It is the chaplain's role to confirm the death and the funeral arrangements before finally passing these details on to the security department to assess the feasibility of the request. The final decision usually lies with the most senior manager on duty in the prison. You might be surprised to hear how many false deaths prisoners have been notified of by people they know outside – often maliciously informed – or how many times chaplains are told by a prisoner that a relative has died in order for them to get an emergency phone call.

Chaplaincy teams can also have responsibility for managing volunteers and linking with community-based faith groups. Whilst most groups and individuals from the community are extremely helpful, there are a few whose mission it appears is to 'save' or 'convert' as many people as they can. Chaplains are not allowed to proselytise but only respond to questions from those not belonging to their faith group. Trying to get this message over to some volunteers can be difficult. Chaplains are sometimes asked by their adherents to help them connect with a local faith group in the community they are returning to. In some cases this role is carried out by the prison's community chaplaincy team if they have one.

My role currently is to operate as a through-the-gate chaplain. In essence, I am a standard Christian chaplain with all the usual endorsements. As stated earlier, I represent the Elim Pentecostal Movement and am licensed to minister as a chaplain. Whilst I occasionally cover for those chaplains who are away, my main function is to support the women on the day of their release from within the prison to the moment they walk through the main gate and for a few minutes afterwards. This is their story as much as it is mine.

'Their' story

*'Nobody gives a **** about me.'* Although this sounds harsh and a little aggressive, this is something I have heard quite a few times, said by women who are just about to leave prison, and something some of them really believe. As an experienced prison chaplain I am very aware of the many challenges that face a person upon their release. We often talk about where they are going to stay, what they may do during the day, how they will find enough money to survive, who's out there to support them and how the person themselves may try to steer clear of trouble. In prison there is a lot of discussion around a prisoner's release, the management of risk and the various levels of support required. We can talk about the importance of people being met as they are released and what happens next. 'Next' in this context can mean the next twenty-four or forty-eight hours.

In the pages that follow I will give a rough outline of how the process may go for the people I support coming out of prison; this may be different in other prisons. My experience is mostly based on working with women coming out of a large women's prison. What I do is rare, possibly unique, and certainly specialist. Meeting women coming out of prison is in itself not unique and there are several organisations that do this and do it very well. But very few specialise in meeting the women who have not signed up to being 'met' and then walking them down to the train station, rubbing shoulders with the general public on the way.

When talking about a woman leaving prison, we very rarely unpack what the first few minutes may be like, what the reality is. We may wish to believe everyone is met at the gate by some 'loving' friend or family member who can't wait to whisk the woman away to a blissful new life. Such a meeting does not always have a 'happy ending'. This book focuses on the women with no one to meet them. Names and one or two scenarios have been slightly altered in order to protect confidentiality and offer privacy. I tend to refer to the released prisoners in this book as 'women'; however the women I walk out through the gate will often refer to themselves as 'girls'. I meet all sorts of women/girls as they are released and begin their journey to the local railway station – to freedom, to a life of hopes and dreams or broken promises and broken hearts, minds that are still behind bars.

The revolving door

For some people, no sooner have we said goodbye to them than we are saying hello again as we see them return and usually in a far worse condition than when they left – having not eaten properly for a while but having consumed huge amounts of illegal substances. Many haven't got anyone to rely on or anyone to meet them as they are released. These are the people I enjoy meeting at the gate, walking with them to the station and sharing a coffee on the platform – when time allows. And why? It is because for just a few minutes I can make a difference. I can't change the world but in the 'here and now' I can offer respect, dignity and a little care, and that can make a huge difference. It can set them up for a better day than they were expecting and some of them may not return as quickly as they have in the past. They may just make their appointments for the day, something they may not have done in the past. Sadly, some people are prone to being abused immediately they are released; Emmy's story highlights this.

Emmy

I met Emmy today, a few minutes after she had been released from prison. I'd seen her inside a few days prior and confirmed I'd meet her as I had done a couple of months earlier. I was on my way back to the prison after having walked with someone else to the station when I spotted Emmy walking down the road, she had just been to the off-licence and bought some loose tobacco and roll-up paper. She was puffing away trying to enjoy her first smoke since being inside for the past twenty-eight days. The prison is 'smoke free' and all the prisoners now have to smoke is a vape, no cigarettes allowed – which is a universal prison policy these days. It was clear the nicotine rush was more than she was expecting. However, having spotted me she waved in my direction and with a quickened step came towards me with her arms open wide. In prison no hugging is allowed between staff and prisoners, but on the out the rules are slightly different and this is the real world; she wanted to greet me on her terms.

Most of the women are released with black holdalls, a sure give-away that they have just come out of prison – but not Emmy. She had come out with no belongings, only her release grant of £46, less than £20 of private money, her medication for anxiety and depression, and her prison issued 'travel warrant' stating her destination, to be exchanged for a train ticket. I knew she was coming out homeless but she had nothing to keep her warm.

Even her coat was torn and this was February – tonight was going to be very cold.

En route to the station Emmy told me what had happened to her shortly after I waved her off at the platform those few weeks ago. She had hooked up with Nats, another woman being released at the same time as her. Emmy was worried as another girl was threatening her and asking for her 'meds' (medication). Nats offered her support and the two were released ahead of the remaining releases that day. I walked with them both and was encouraged by Nats' wisdom and obvious appreciation of how vulnerable Emmy was. As Emmy was NFA (of No Fixed Abode), Nats offered to give her a sofa for the night and said she'd see that she was okay. I waved them off, wishing them well. But things changed almost immediately the train doors closed. Nats was NFA too but had somewhere she was heading towards and invited Emmy to join her. When they had travelled past a few stations they got off together. Emmy was now in a town she didn't know. Nats was heading to the home of an 'old man' who would look after her in return for sexual favours. She told Emmy that he wanted a threesome and would pay £60, of which she could have half. At this Emmy parted company with Nats, but only after Nats had taken everything she had – including the few clothes she had been given outside. I had considered 'From Prison to Prostitution' as a sub-title for this section, as that is the reality for some – either they are going back to what they know or being led into it for the first time.

Emmy was now in a strange place, homeless, with no money or medication. She had missed her probation appointment and was totally alone. She resorted to sleeping in doorways and begging. One 'kind lady' took her into a local baker's and bought her something to eat. For the next few days the bakery gave her food and drink. On one occasion when begging she asked a man for money; his response was to smack her in the mouth! At that point she gave up and rang the police from a payphone, stating she thought she had a warrant out for her arrest. When they arrived, they confirmed the outstanding warrant, but first took her to hospital as they suspected her jaw had been broken. Thankfully, it hadn't been, but of course she was returned to prison.

Although I have no way of verifying Emmy's story, it was consistent with what I know happens to the homeless and those people who are vulnerable when leaving prison. I listened and said how sad it was that this had happened to her. It sounded awful and as there was no gain in her lying, I believe it happened just as she said. We made our way to the station; she exchanged her travel warrant for a ticket and was given directions as to what trains to catch to get her to her destination. Her plan was to report to Probation as directed and then head off to a church to find some support. At some point she was going to get her methadone script and plan where she might sleep for the night. As I waved her off, she and I both knew we could be doing this again in a few weeks' time.

I'm not sure if this was a better 'send-off' from the platform than the previous time I had waved Emmy goodbye. At least last time she had hope. Of course, it didn't last long, but for a few minutes she had real hope that someone would take care of her, that she would have a bed for the night and that she would be safe. This time she had little hope that tonight she was going to be safe, that anybody really cared and that she could avoid coming back to prison. All I can say is that for the hour we spent together she was safe; she knew I cared about her and was wishing her well. From me there was no judgement, no false hope, only an appreciation that life 'sucks' at times.

Reflection

Luke 23:44-46

It was now about noon, and darkness came over the whole land until three in the afternoon, for the sun stopped shining. And the curtain of the temple was torn in two. Jesus called out with a loud voice, 'Father, into your hands I commit my spirit.' When he had said this, he breathed his last.

When the budgie hits the fan

Jesus' journey that week had taken him from crowds cheering him as he entered Jerusalem to the agony and pain of dying on the cross. Whilst most of us will never experience those extremes, some of us can identify with things that appear to go downhill. Many of the women I work with will share their story with me. In some cases life is going along well, then something happens, like being made unemployed or the loss of someone close to them or they become friends with someone who leads them down a path they didn't even know existed. As the saying goes, 'One thing leads to another,' and before they knew it they were involved in something out of their control which eventually led them into prison. For some this can be a quick journey and yet for others it's a long, slow path downwards. Their journey is one of pain and confusion. 'This was not how life was meant to be,' some might think. I often describe this experience as 'When the budgie hits the fan'. Many of us can relate to this phrase. We can imagine just what it means when something goes horribly wrong and there is 'mess' and 'carnage' all around us. I have used this expression many times in prison and nearly everyone understands what it means and what it might look like for them. One day I was talking to a prisoner and used this same analogy. But she took it further and said, *'When that happens you need to pick up the feathers and make a pillow.'* Thanks, MJ. I think she's spot-on. However, in reality it would take a lot of 'feathers' to make a 'pillow', but there again, some of us have had a lot of experience with unsuspecting budgies. The secret is trying to make the best out of whatever comes our way.

It could be said that for the two on the Emmaus road the 'budgie hit the fan' when Jesus was crucified, or for the Samaritan woman – who had previously had five husbands before she met Jesus at the well – there were at least five 'budgies' that got too close to the 'fan'. What they all have in common is that they made the 'best' of their encounters with Jesus. I try and make the best of the short time I have with the women. It is my hope that they see something of the 'love' of Jesus in me as we journey together, at whatever point in our journeys that is. Unfortunately, the two people on the road to Emmaus weren't at the point of seeing anything good coming out of what had happened. All they could see was carnage – Jesus had just been crucified and they were in shock!

Questions

1. Can you remember a situation that occurred and left you in shock, but is now resolved?

2. How did you feel?
3. How did it get resolved?
4. Did anyone assist you at that time?

For prayer

Sadly, many of the people who come out of prison are still in shock and feel they are failures; they can't see how things can get better and believe there is no one around who can help them. Please pray for all those who have experienced 'the budgie hitting the fan', including people you may know and those coming out of prison.

Chapter 2
Waiting To Be Released

The pre-release process

I'm the bag carrier. 'He carries your bag to the station,' she says in a validating way. What she's saying in reality is 'he's a good guy', and that means a lot to me. She's a prisoner on the cusp of being released and waiting with the others in the holding cell just prior to the completion of paperwork and only minutes from walking out of the jail and back into the community. She can't remember my name and I can't remember hers but we both know we've been here before. The holding cell in our prison is a room that hosts eleven soft plastic fabricated armchairs in a white painted room with two coffee-style tables and a television mounted in the corner. It has two windows with the uniform bars and grills to let in any air; the outlook is concrete. I introduce myself to the others and tell them that I'm a through-the-gate chaplain who meets the women just before they get out and, if they want, I walk them to the train station, carrying their bags if it helps. She nods with approval and authority. Having her endorse what I do could make a huge difference to how the next forty-five minutes will turn out. Yet sadly, by the time we leave the holding cell located in the discharge area of the prison, any ringing endorsement of the help I offer can be lost and various plans made over the past few weeks can be completely undone by what sometimes occurs in that cell. New-found good intentions and much thought can be lost in a matter of minutes if the prisoner's thoughts are waylaid by old unhelpful thoughts coming back and taking centre stage in their mind. Some women are very quick to turn down my offer of help, usually because they want to head straight to the off-licence in the local shop at the end of the road and don't want anyone slowing them down – especially a 'do-goody vicar' (I'm not a vicar, by the way). I smile and then inform them that once they've got their 'can' and cigarettes, they may want me to hold their bags as they walk to the station. It's like I've just read their mind and my 'fan' from earlier pipes up with, 'I told you he's OK.'

In most cases the person being released is aware of their release date some time in advance and has given some if not a lot of thought to it. A few days after they have arrived in custody they are issued with a document which states the date they are to be released as well as when their sentence is completed. It may also state what date they are eligible for Home Detention Curfew, known as HDC or more commonly referred to as 'the tag'. This is an electronic devise affixed usually to a person's ankle which transmits a signal and is activated at night when the person should be at a specific location whilst under a curfew. If the signal is broken then this may be because the person has left the location without permission and could be recalled to prison. A large number of people are released around halfway through their sentence and remain on licence in the community for the remainder of the time. This may alter if the person has been recalled to prison having failed to comply with their original licence conditions.

Prior to a person's release it is good practice for a plan to be put in place for when the person returns to the community. Various people can be involved in this process, including their supervising probation officer or Community Rehabilitation Company (CRC) officer based in the area they are returning to. Also involved can be an internal prison-based CRC officer, the Integrated Offender Management Unit (IOMU) supervisor, case workers representing drug and alcohol services, healthcare professionals, specialist workers who can assist is areas such as domestic abuse and sex working when relevant. The prisoner's family may also be consulted during this period, especially if the person is going to reside with them when released. Whilst the prisoner is the central figure in this plan, the irony is that they don't always have much say in what is being planned. This can be because the options are very limited – there is only one place where they can reside or that, due to the nature of their offence, there are statutory conditions they have to adhere to regardless as to whether they want to or not. The ideal is that these plans are arranged weeks in advance of the prisoner's release, so everyone knows what is going to happen and what is expected of them. They may have been able to arrange for someone to pick them up from the gate and be aware of any appointments they have that day. For some women their stay in prison has been a shock and they vow this is the first and last time they will come to prison and have engaged fully in their prison experience, attending courses and complying with everything asked of them, while others just do the bare essentials.

For those who have received a short sentence of only a few weeks, although some thought may have been given to the process, unfortunately little action has taken place because of the tight timescale. And if the person leaving has a complicated and chaotic lifestyle, then they may have left things to the last minute and still be packing moments before they are on their way to the last stage before release.

This stage includes the signing of various documents such as the person's licence, reporting instructions (to their CRC or probation) and fire arms documentation, as well as signing for their belongings, money and valuables. All this should be checked carefully in front of them. They may also be issued with a travel warrant. Occasionally I have witnessed prison officers hand over money to the prisoner in such a way that other prisoners can see how much they are receiving. The experienced 'old timer' will then look for their opportunity to help themselves or ask for a 'loan'; they may even suggest that two of them 'buddy up' on the journey out of town, hoping for a handout later or even the chance to rob the one with the money if it's a lot and worth the risk.

Things can also go wrong for people when they find they do not have as much money upon release as they were expecting, or that some of their belongings they thought were in prison in 'stored prop' (property withheld by the prison until they are released) are not there, or they are told they are not getting all the medication they thought they were due or they have to report somewhere they weren't expecting to.

Kezi

I met Kezi at the counter in the reception area of the prison. She was somewhat animated given she had just found out that she had to report to a probation team in an area she needed to keep away from. Her caseworker was trying to support her in her frustrated state and explore with her the options. Thankfully Kezi 'held it together' and didn't become angry. Finally she left and was met at the gate by two through-the-gate workers and joined by her prison caseworker. Further confusion followed and the caseworker went back inside the prison to make a few more phone calls, all four of us headed off to the Community Coffee Shop just outside the prison gate. Eventually the caseworker joined us with a revised plan of action which appeared to appease Kezi. However, she still had money in the prison she was waiting for so, after a phone call was made, she and I wandered back to the gatehouse and eventually picked up her earnings. On the way back to the coffee shop I praised Kezi for the way she had controlled herself. She said that in the past she would have 'lost it', got very angry and who knows what she would have done. I highlighted how far she had come and how proud I was of the way she had managed herself in such a challenging situation. A huge smile came across her face and she thanked me for recognising how she had handled herself. As she went to walk off with the support workers, she asked if I was a Christian – knowing that I was a chaplain. When I said I was she replied, 'I thought so, I'm a Christian too,' and off she went. Sometimes all it takes is a little praise and recognition to bring out a smile and set people up for a positive next step.

Final checks

One of the last stages is a final ID check by a manager, ensuring the right person is being released. For many people working in the prison system, the practical and business side of release is what constitutes release process, but for those being released there is an emotional and mental one as well as the technical aspect to their release. There can often be a lot of tension at this time of waiting and a lot of impatience from prisoners and staff alike! Some people sit there quietly, waiting their turn to go up to the counter and get their belongings, while others pace up and down. There's often one person who is loud and very excitable and one person who makes it clear they can't stand them! There is a real mix of backgrounds, races, academic ability, life skills and relationships. It's not unusual to hear the women talk about their boy or girlfriends and what they are hoping for from their partners when they are released. Some hope they will meet them with drugs, while others talk of the sex they are going to have that night. Some women have boyfriends 'at home' but 'girlfriends' when they are behind bars, within the prison. Women who prefer same sex relationships are very common in prison, as well as people who have 'transgendered'. So the talk of sex is quite common in the holding cell as is the talk of revenge! Some women wonder if their partner has been faithful, while others have heard rumours that they haven't been and are going to make them 'pay' or get as far away from them as they can.

For several days the person may have been reminding themselves of what they need to do upon release, self-talking themselves into a positive state, focusing on a changed life: new opportunities and a new hope. Then, at the last minute, nerves begin to kick in: 'What if my lift is not there or the place where I am hoping to stay won't have me? What am I going to do for money?' Concerns about broken relationships may come to the surface as the clock ticks down. All this can be unsettling as the person awaits their release on that 'special' day.

In this fragile state vulnerable people are at risk of being coerced into dropping their plans and adopting ones placed in front of them by someone purporting to be their mate. 'Hello, babes,' one woman says to another as they meet in the holding cell. 'I didn't know you was coming out today.' Whenever I hear 'Hello, babes' my heart sinks. I can almost recite the script. The conversation starts subtly, with a few questions about where they may be heading. Then they are asked if they are going to 'score' – look for drugs – and asked if they have been looking forward to 'using'. These are thoughts some will have had but fought hard to put behind them, yet now someone is bringing them to the fore and in an enticing way. Or it may be that someone gets alongside another person who is obviously unsure of where they are going that night – they may have an option of family but they don't always get on with them. Then their 'new mate' offers them a place for the night and all their plans change, including reporting that day.

It is here that conditioning – 'befriending' with an ulterior motive, usually for personal gain – takes place as someone offers the soon to be released person contraband or an item of clothing with apparently 'no strings attached'. Yet later, when they are through the gate, something may be asked of them – a favour! When the women have all their belongings they will pack and repack their bags several times and it is at this point that more 'trading', the swapping of belongings, can take place. Amidst all the packing it is easy for a woman to lose her travel warrant or mislay valuables. Experienced women are always on the lookout for a first-timer who leaves her bag unattended. Confused, conditioned and vulnerable people are waiting alongside the experienced and cunning, as prey to the predator and often with no one in sight to stop the inevitable panning out.

Scared

The holding cell can be full of very scared people and that includes the predators. Sometimes I think a few people set themselves up to fail because then they are in control of their situation. 'Come on, Sim, you know what I'm going to do when I'm out.' I've heard that a good few times. And I do know. I know they are going to be looking for drugs, going back to their 'old mates' to do what they do. I value their openness and honesty and sometimes we can have a really good conversation, especially when no one else is around. There are always a few who think they know best, do things their way and can win against their 'demons' even if the 'demon' is sat in front of them with one arm tied behind its back – sadly the 'demon' often wins the battle, even if it has only one hand, one leg and one eye. I remember thinking as a youngster that I knew best and that joining the Army was the right thing for me to do. However, I'm sure my parents had significant doubts, as did my friends, especially as I had up until the year before I left school shown no particular interest in the military, never even fired a rifle at a funfair. Yet there I was ploughing on with my idea, listening to no one. I entered Ouston barracks in Northumberland in the September and left in the December of the same year with my Army career over. Thankfully it wasn't a disastrous mistake, unlike some I've seen.

When the holding cell begins to fill up the dynamics begin to change. This is when bravado kicks in, and it has a big kick! Personas have to be kept up and suddenly an honest and open person changes into a 'street lingo styled gangster'. Words trip off their tongue and sometimes I have no idea what they are saying. Then the whispering starts and little cliques develop and I know plans are being altered, tailored to the new players.

I sit in the corner of the room, now excluded from the conversation yet quietly offering up a few silent prayers. After a few moments I weigh up my next move, looking to see if there is anyone presenting as particularly vulnerable – someone who appears uncomfortable. If I spot them I'll often go over and make small talk, finding out if this is their first time being released and hear about their plans for the day. Depending on their response I may just wish them well and leave it at that. Yet some people show signs of really appreciating my enquiry and it's then that I may offer to assist them as they leave. Some people are guarded at first, then open up and are very engaging, yet others give off an aura of 'keep away from me or I'll thump you'. Being able to read these signals is rather important. If I'm too imposing that can put people off and if I'm too laid back I can miss an opportunity to help. My eyes and ears are always open – alert to what is going on, keeping an eye on unattended bags and vulnerable people. I often find it better when the experienced prisoner is kept separated from the first-timer. So many times I've heard the old-timer reassuringly offer support to the uninitiated newbie and it being gratefully received; sadly, I know in my heart how this is going to end. Sometimes I just have to stand back because interfering could cause more trouble, with all sorts of allegations flying around. However, sometimes I can grab a quiet word with the newcomer and offer a gentle warning as to what may occur – I have shared 'Emmy's story' with a few people.

Being met

If I hear that a woman is being met by someone then I let her know that if they are not at the prison by the time she is released, then she can wait in the Visitor Reception Centre where there is the Community Coffee Shop and there she can get a hot drink while she waits. This is provided free of charge for all those being released. The coffee shop is a safe place for people to wait, keep warm and collect their thoughts.

Just because people are being met doesn't necessarily mean that all is going to go well. I remember the case of a woman who I met in the holding cell prior to being released. I couldn't have a detailed conversation with her as English was her second language and she didn't understand much of what I was saying. However, she made it clear she was expecting someone to meet her and this clearly made her happy – lots of smiles. As the gate finally rolled back you could see she was extremely pleased to see her partner, so pleased that she ran towards him, just like in the romantic movies. Yet what happened next took me by surprise. Instead of him breaking into a jog to meet her half way he remained fixed – some way in the distance, in an arms-folded position. Alongside him was a teenage boy who stood a pace or two behind him. As the woman got closer to the man she slowed down; she obviously knew him well enough to know that all was not good but not well enough to think that he wouldn't be pleased to see her – and he wasn't pleased at all! She stopped with bags in hand, about three paces in front of him, like a naughty student in front of the teacher, her head slightly bowed as he 'read her the riot act'. I didn't need to know the language to know that he was extremely angry and felt justified in laying down the law. The boy stood quietly behind him, no doubt he knew that this was coming and he, too, knew his place. As I walked by I couldn't help feel sorry for the woman as she appeared not only surprised but shell shocked; this was certainly not the greeting she'd been dreaming of. Eventually the boy took the bags and they all got into a car. I know nothing of what happened next. Perhaps this became a 'happy ever after' story, with a clearing of the air and a romantic making-up session later that night – but I doubt it. Perhaps when they got home she got the physical beating he thought she deserved but wouldn't administer in public. Or perhaps nothing more was said of her time in prison and everything went back to how it was before or . . . And that's just it; very often we don't know what happens next.

People can go off happily together only for things to break down in their relationship. A couple of months ago I waved off a woman I knew well. She had been met by her parents and was talking positively about having a new start. A few weeks later I was waving her off again at the station. It transpires that things did not go well between her and her parents, she breached her licence conditions and was recalled to prison for fourteen days.

When people tell me they are being met I sometimes ask if this is a good thing.

Head-rush

Now with most of the business formalities done, anticipation, anxiety, hope and helplessness are mixed together as the releases walk to the exit – 'the gate'. One last check of ID, then the gate is rolled back or the door is unlocked. This is perhaps the most critical moment in the whole process. Some people are met with smiles and hugs; others are left to their own devices. However, just because someone is hugged, it does not mean they are loved.

It is now that some of the released people can be clearly identified with black bags in hand, linking up as they walk to the transport. In some cases they will head straight away to the local shop, almost running to get their first cigarette for a while and, with it, a 'head-rush' moment. Here they may also be able to buy their first celebratory 'drink'. Some prisons have good public transport links, like mine. However, some are in remote places where prison-organised transport may be required, sometimes a minibus to the local town. Sadly, some never get out of 'my' town sober or crime free. Some released people come out without any money, so the first thing they do is shoplift.

Some people do not have any time to stop and reflect; they are full steam ahead! Others go more slowly, trying to process where they are and where they need to get to. And then there are those who do not want to think about things; for some the thoughts are too painful. Of course, there are those who are going back to settled environments, to catch up with positive influences in their lives, but sadly for some the days of 'happy families' are well in the past, so hearing others around them talk about such things can really frustrate or upset them. This is when the 'why bother' self-talk steps up a pace. Journeying with someone can be good for them, as being distracted is what is required at that precise moment. Unfortunately some 'paths' are easy to stray from, especially in the wrong company. Often the only people who really 'get' how the released person feels are those who have been there themselves.

Just as there is a chemical reaction to the first cigarette, so there is an emotional reaction to being released. The initial joy as the gate pulls back can soon be replaced by depression, of feeling alone, abandoned. The longer the journey, the more opportunity there is to think the 'dark' thoughts. Remaining positive can be a real struggle.

Reflection

Luke 24:1-8

On the first day of the week, very early in the morning, the women took the spices they had prepared and went to the tomb. They found the stone rolled away from the tomb, but when they entered, they did not find the body of the Lord Jesus. While they were wondering about this, suddenly two men in clothes that gleamed like lightning stood beside them. In their fright the women bowed down with their faces to the ground, but the men said to them, 'Why do you look for the living among the dead? He is not here; he has risen! Remember how he told you, while he was still with you in Galilee: "The Son of Man must be delivered over to the hands of sinners, be crucified and on the third day be raised again."' Then they remembered his words.

Luke 24:13-16

Now that same day two of them were going to a village called Emmaus, about seven miles from Jerusalem. They were talking with each other about everything that had happened. As they talked and discussed these things with each other, Jesus himself came up and walked along with them; but they were kept from recognising him.

The wrong direction

Jesus has died and there is confusion all around. Reports are beginning to circulate that the tomb is empty and even people are saying that he is alive! The majority of the disciples and followers of Jesus are together in Jerusalem, probably trying to figure out what is going on and comforting each other. But not our two on the road to Emmaus; they are walking away from the 'action', away from their friends and away from the answers.

Every time I preach from this passage I can't help thinking these two are heading in the wrong direction! They have spent many months with Jesus, they would have heard him talk about who he is and his mission here on earth. Yet they are walking away! Are they cowards running away from the 'heat' of the situation or just confused and needing to clear their heads? Of course there may be a third reason – they needed to get back for a birthday party. As frivolous and whimsical as this sounds, and as you know I do like whimsy, it might just be that there was a very clear reason why they had to be back at home in Emmaus at that particular time and maybe they had delayed their return due to everything that was happening in Jerusalem. Perhaps one of them wanted to go back and persuaded the other to join them, who knows? We also don't know at what point Jesus joined them, how far along the road they were.

Whatever their reason was for making the journey, it still appears they were in deep discussion and unable to recognise

Jesus, who was probably the last person they were expecting to see, even though he had told them he was going to overcome death. They had been given information that should have made it clear as to what was going on and perhaps shaped their thinking and even prompted them to remain with the others in hope and expectation.

Many of the people I work with have been given information that should enable them to make clearly informed decisions. Yet still many of them head in what appears to be the opposite direction. They enter the holding cell armed with information about where they should go, who they should meet, where they may stay and what they could be doing in the next few days. However, whilst waiting, a few people are tempted to drop their original plans and deliberately 'forget' the information they have been given and leave the prison with others who may not be particularly helpful.

One of the amazing things about this passage is that, upon meeting them, Jesus didn't say, 'Hey folks, it's me,' and show them his hands. That could have saved everybody a long walk and, let's face it, he must have been exhausted! What energy! What patience! What love!

Questions

1. Has there been a time in your life when you have been heading in the wrong direction and chosen to ignore good advice?
2. How did it turn out?
3. Would you do things differently if faced with the same choices again?

4. Do you know others who are heading in the wrong direction too?

For prayer

Some of the women I meet in the holding cell know that what they are about to do is against all the good advice they have been given, yet they still do it and do it several times more. Please pray for those people heading in the wrong direction, that they may take notice of advice given them.

Chapter 3
From The Gate To The Local Shop

The main gate

The main gate is a huge wooden door, large enough to let all shapes and sizes of vehicles through, and when it rolls back all is revealed. By this time I have already left the women; as they walk from the discharge area to the main gate, I go on ahead of them so that when they walk through the gate I am outside waiting for them. Sometimes I stand back and watch the drama unfold. 'Hello, babes,' the unwanted boyfriend says to his shocked 'girl', her reply being, 'What the **** are you doing here?' 'Fort I'd surprise you,' is his romantic reply. I try not to listen in to anything more, it can be painful.

Some of the women being released are looking around anxiously trying to spot their 'lift', while others run into the arms of their loved ones. Tears, swearing and silence all hover in the air. There is so much emotion at the gate, so much drama, pain and joy.

Some women have 'professionals' to meet them, people from organisations that support women through the gate; often they have met the woman before her release, a risk assessment has been carried out and an agreement signed, stating what is going to happen and the behaviour that is expected. Then the woman is escorted to wherever has been identified for her, which may be an appointment with her caseworker or probation officer, an agreed hostel or the council housing department.

By the time the women come out I usually have an idea of who I might be supporting. It's not uncommon for a woman to make it clear to me while we are waiting inside that she would like my help, but even at the gate her mind may change. Sometimes an officer or a CRC worker may also ask me to support someone. On some occasions it's more of a loose arrangement with the woman seemingly not fussed as to whether I support her or not. The women I tend to link up with are those who are alone and unsupported on this occasion. The majority of these women have declined any offer of help or have no one available who can meet them on that particular day. Maybe they don't want to be tied down by a through-the-gate worker who could apply a little pressure to conform to the previously agreed plan, which they now want to ditch. Or they know exactly where they are going and again don't want anyone trying to talk them out of it. I have also walked with people who just don't have anyone to collect them. This is sometimes due to the distance their elderly parent may have to drive or because all the people who would want to assist them are working or otherwise engaged. Sometimes it's just too short notice to arrange something.

'Hi, I'm a not a dealer . . .'

Just occasionally I meet a woman for the first time as she comes through the gate. This may be because I have already walked some people down to the station and the woman now coming out was late getting to the discharge area, perhaps because she was still packing, showering, finishing putting on her make-up or just waiting to say goodbye to friends and the officer collecting her from the house block to take her over to the discharge area couldn't wait any longer. *'Hi, I'm not a dealer, I'm a chaplain and I meet the women coming out who are walking to the station.'* These are my first words I greet her with and then show my ID. Sometimes the woman recognises me and sometimes she looks blankly back at me. I'm usually dressed in practical clothing, ready for walking to the station, wearing trainers, a thick coat or T-shirt depending on the weather – but not a clerical collar. Once they've seen my ID, I go on to explain that I am happy to walk with them to the station. At this point one of two things usually happens: either they say, 'No, thank you, I'm alright,' and walk on at a great pace, or they stop and listen to my offer as it unfolds. I go on to explain that I can show her the way to the station, perhaps even help carry her bag. Whatever the response, I normally let them know that I'm likely to end up at the station, even if it's not with her but someone else. It's always easier if they have seen me inside; some women are wisely wary of me as they know that dealers have been known to hang around the area, while some women are disappointed I'm not a dealer!

Yes, please

Those women who accept my support are often anxious and appreciate the assistance. Some people accept my offer because they are suspicious of the other women going to the station and want protection from them or even from themselves, especially from caving in to their cravings for alcohol, which is as readily available at 9.30am in the morning – or even earlier – as it is at 9.30pm in the evening in at least two places en route to the station.

And of course the off-licences don't want to refuse to sell their alcohol to people who want to buy it, even if it is going to send them straight back to the practice of their addiction. After the woman is sure I am who I purport to be, she accepts my company and off we walk. If they are coatless I sometimes offer to pop into the Visitor Reception Centre which is just outside the prison gate and see if we can find one from the spare clothing stored there for this exact purpose. There we encounter the prison's Community Coffee Shop which serves quality coffee, teas of all flavours and hot chocolate – hot chocolate is a favourite with a large number of the women and some still add sugar. In fact most add sugar to any drink and plenty of it. I've normally explained in the holding cell that the drink is free, so the women have already decided what they want, and what they want is usually a better taste than the decaffeinated 'brew' they are used to inside. However, there are still women who ask how much it is, in order to see if they can afford it.

No, thank you

Usually this is said quite firmly as the woman passes by me as fast as she possibly can. I don't take this personally as it's not so much about me but more the fact that she wants to get to the local shop as quick as she can. She knows what she is doing and she knows what she wants. She also knows she doesn't want anyone slowing her down or getting in the way. That is also the case if she is on the look-out for a pre-arranged drug dealer. This happened not so long ago when a woman I knew very well from the past – Zoe – politely refused my offer and made it clear she was looking for someone. As it turned out she didn't look too hard and eventually got to the station without doing the deal she'd been planning. We both knew who and what she was looking for – drugs. She told me she knew it wasn't the best thing for her and as she had a Christian faith knew it wasn't what God wanted for her either. She walked briskly ahead of me, but then slowed down. She appeared to look around a little but was in my eyesight all the time. Then she came to a stop and waited for me to catch up with her; I was walking with some other women by that time. It was her choice not to do a thorough search but I think me being around was a nudge in the right direction. That was a success and I was proud of her, which I told her when I saw her back inside a couple of weeks later. Yup, she only lasted a few weeks outside but she could have been back within a few days had she succumbed to the temptation earlier. There is no point in trying to slow anyone down or dissuading them from their mission. I have found it easier to just let them speed off, and perhaps catch up with them later.

Down the drive

It's very common for the women to give a cheer as they step from the shadows of the prison to 'freedom'. Some are superstitious and believe that looking back towards the gate will bring bad luck; some might say it's a little late for that. So looking ahead, straight down the drive, the women fix their eyes in front of them, looking for people or to see if they can spot the shop which they know is down the end there somewhere. However, after only a few metres they stop and begin asking anyone around if they have a light for a stale cigarette they've found in their belongings or found in someone else's. To prevent visitors or staff from being accosted by very excitable people desperate for their first smoke in weeks or even months, I carry a lighter on me. I don't smoke and never have but know this simple act of offering a light can calm some nerves. This also slows down their desire to get to the shop at the end of the drive and 'a can with their name on it', figuratively speaking. I keep the lighter in a bag which I keep in the Visitor Reception Centre.

Bag of 'tricks'

I usually retrieve my bag just before the women come out of the prison and let the barista in the coffee shop know that the women are on their way out and how many of them may be popping in for their free drink. In my bag I have a cap and gloves for if the weather is looking a bit glum, and a mobile phone. I also have tissues, give-away Gideon New Testament Bibles, Rosary Beads, cards with Bible texts or useful sayings on them and occasionally an Islamic book of prayer. As previously stated, it is not the role of a chaplain to convert people to their particular faith but we are to bring comfort and support to those of the same faith. All of the women know I'm part of the chaplaincy team and most know that we have something to do with God or religion, even if they don't know what chaplaincy means. Some will disclose they are believers of one sort or another. If they make it known they are Christian I will ask what denomination they belong to or which church, if any, they attend. Unfortunately many don't exactly know; they say, 'I go to Saint . . .' and expect me to know it or some don't even know the name but will have a go at trying to describe it. Those who are Roman Catholic know they are RC and if they are not wearing a Rosary I will ask them if they would like one. Most of the women are very grateful and some even ask me to bless it. I make it clear to them that I am not a priest and that they should go find an RC priest to do it. However, I will offer to pray for them and offer a general blessing. When I have Islamic material I will offer it to those who are Muslim. I offer these items because for some it brings them comfort and helps them connect to their faith. It also helps me engage better with them as they can see I respect their faith or belief system.

Risk assessments

As I mentioned earlier, most of the women who have a through-the-gate worker or professional will have undergone various assessments. One of these would have been a risk assessment in order to ascertain what risks the woman might pose to the person escorting them. Yet because I meet these women 'cold' – without background information and without even knowing their name until I introduce myself – no formal risk assessment has been carried out. So I do an on-the-spot dynamic risk assessment. I ask the officers who are in the discharge area if they know them, and invariably they do, so I ask them for a little background information. Then I look at how they interact with the officers and the other prisoners, looking for any odd behaviours such as repetitive conversation, eyes not focusing and lack of concentration. From having a brief conversation with a woman I can gauge how 'balanced' she presents, given that it's natural to be stressed when released, especially if they don't know where they are staying that night. If we have met before then I can compare how she presents this time with previous times. There is at least one woman who always presents a little oddly – this is consistent behaviour and I'd be more worried if she didn't have the fixed stare she usually has. If I'm uncomfortable with the way someone presents then I limit what support I offer, however I have only done this a few times. This means I may not be there to meet them when they walk through the gate on the outside or I'll only go to the coffee shop with them. I usually tell them if I'm unable to escort them to the railway station but I don't always tell them why?

Even if I'm happy about walking to the station I still have safety measures in place. I am trained in personal protection and carry a phone with me at all times. I also have 'safe houses' along the way – places I can pop into if I'm feeling vulnerable. These are the coffee shop, the off-licence/local shop at the end of the drive, two churches and the train station ticket office area. I can talk to any of the staff working in these places if I need assistance.

Risks

If there is need of a risk assessment then what are the risks? Whilst I have a concern as to what risks the women coming out may pose to each other, my main concern is how safe am I? If I am to walk to the station with someone I barely know then I have to be confident that I'm not going to be abused and even stolen from. Most women I walk alongside pose no threat to me or the public and if they did they wouldn't be released in the normal way.

However, on one occasion I was with a group of women in the holding cell and one of them was someone I had upset in the past. Previously she had got on a train with someone who didn't present as being 'helpful', even though she was supposed to be met at the prison. I'd had a call from the prison saying that her lift had turned up and had been directed to find me at the station. I informed her 'lift' she had left and in what circumstances. Apparently this got her into trouble later. She had remembered this and shared it with a couple who were also waiting to be released. They were overheard plotting to rob me on her behalf and I was informed. So when we got to the coffee shop I told them I was staying there and would not be journeying with them further. Ironically, on this occasion the woman waited for her lift, so I feel what I did previously did have a positive impact, although not for me. Apart from that incident I haven't been threatened.

The Community Coffee Shop

My first safe haven or 'safe house' is the Community Coffee Shop in the Visitor Reception Centre, still on prison grounds and about a third of the way down the short drive to the main road leading to the railway station. It's in the coffee shop that I meet up with any volunteers who may be assisting me that day and I have a few who help me each week. The lure of a free drink pulls quite a few women in. Sometimes it's a safe place to wait for the woman's 'lift'. Yesterday a woman came out and her friend was half an hour away from meeting her as she had got caught in traffic. The woman talked to me and the volunteer whilst waiting. It transpired that she has an alcohol problem and that it had contributed to her coming into prison and not for the first time. Just prior to being collected she thanked us for staying and talking to her. She said that had it not been for us she would have walked down the road and purchased some alcohol from the off-licence. This time she was leaving the area absolutely sober, unlike last time.

Often, I find that women who while waiting in the holding cell have spoken about getting a 'can' of their preferred flavour from the off-licence, decide that they no longer have the same need once they're holding a nice cup of latte, cappuccino or hot chocolate and are quite happy to walk past the off-licence without popping in, especially if they don't need to buy cigarettes.

To the off-licence/local shop

We live in a culture where it is common to celebrate anything with a drink of alcohol, even if it's 9.00am in the morning and especially if you have been released from prison and all you've been thinking about is that first 'drink'. Some women are so focused on that drink that they walk straight past the coffee shop; they may pause, however, to say goodbye to a member of staff who is walking down the drive. In their excitement I have heard several women tell staff they know or even people they don't know that they are 'free'. This might be a little obvious but none the less they feel it needs to be said or even shouted! Whilst this is true – in that they are out of prison and free to go on their way – the prison still has a duty of care for those released up to twenty-four hours post release. If they die within that time period post their release, this is still viewed as a 'death in custody' and the prison will be involved in any coroner's inquest. Oblivious to this, the women march on to their 'prize' and reward themselves for surviving prison – that celebratory drink. Along the way they may rip open sealed bags that have contained their mobile phones and money. The bags that have their names and prison number on them are then discarded and dropped on the ground as a testimony that 'Ms Smith was here'.

Reflection

Luke 24:17-24

He asked them, 'What are you discussing together as you walk along?'

They stood still, their faces downcast. One of them, named Cleopas, asked him, 'Are you the only one visiting Jerusalem who does not know the things that have happened there in these days?'

'What things?' he asked.

'About Jesus of Nazareth,' they replied. 'He was a prophet, powerful in word and deed before God and all the people. The chief priests and our rulers handed him over to be sentenced to death, and they crucified him; but we had hoped that he was the one who was going to redeem Israel. And what is more, it is the third day since all this took place. In addition, some of our women amazed us. They went to the tomb early this morning but didn't find his body. They came and told us that they had seen a vision of angels, who said he was alive. Then some of our companions went to the tomb and found it just as the women had said, but they did not see Jesus.'

Listen to this . . .

The two on the road to Emmaus were so full of woe and dejected that not only did they not recognise Jesus, they actually showed dismay that this other traveller did not know what had been happening back there in Jerusalem. Jesus could have been a little annoyed that they didn't recognise him. Yet instead of him stopping them in full flow and telling them it was he they were talking to, he asked them a couple of questions and listened to them as they shared their hopes, despair and confusion. He gave them space to let it all out!

Much of my time spent with the women is focused around me listening to them and giving them space to tell me whatever they want me to hear. They, too, share some of their hopes – hope for a changed life, hope that this time they can stay 'clean', hope that there is someone waiting for them, hope that they won't be alone or back in prison again. They will also share their despair with how things have worked out, despair with themselves at how they have been unable to 'kick the habit' and let themselves and others down; despair at how they are estranged from their children and despair at what support really is out there for them upon their release. Some just don't know how it is all going to work out, when or if they'll ever get their life back together again.

I, too, remember wondering if I was ever going to reach what I was hoping for – a family, children, a nice home and a good job; after all, for years I had been told this was beyond me. And even when life started to go in the right direction, even then I doubted it would last or 'end' well for me. I had such low self-esteem and a lack of self-confidence that I couldn't see myself marrying, having children and getting the dream job. Eventually I met my wife and the children came along, we had a nice home and my career prospects were on the up. However, I still struggled with self-confidence, especially regarding my academic ability, and this fed into insecurities and my self-esteem, which although higher than before was still not where it could have been. It wasn't until my mid-twenties to mid-thirties that things began to change. In that ten-year period things began to click into place. I felt God begin to heal me from my doubts and fears, although I still had battles and wasn't always the greatest of husbands and fathers back then. I remember one scripture hit me; it was the first time I came across Psalm 139, especially verse 14: *'I praise you because I am fearfully and wonderfully made.'* I remember who introduced me to it and where I was at the time. That really got to me! 'Could I say, "I'm wonderfully made," as David had; could I own that too?' Eventually I did and came to celebrate the uniqueness of me and value the thought that my disability had help shape me into the person I was and am to this day. Not only was I encouraged by scripture at that time but by several people around me, including my wife Julie and various friends. One such person was Jan who was a psychotherapist and my external supervisor when I worked with people with learning disabilities. She listened to me and skilfully reflected back things she knew would help me grow both as a person and as a skilled practitioner in my work place. I doubt if she ever thought she would be likened to Jesus but that is exactly what Jesus did on the Emmaus road: he listened and then fed back.

Questions

1. Can you reflect upon a time when you felt hopeless and unsure as to how things were going to work out, but somehow they did?
2. Can you remember what caused the change of feelings?
3. Can you recall a time when you were there to listen to others who were struggling with personal issues?
4. When you listened – how did that make them feel?

For prayer

I once asked a woman what was the one thing she would like to see changed that would help her as she resettles back into the community. Her answer wasn't what I expected and took me by surprise: she said she wanted more time in her appointments with the various professionals she had to engage with, so they had more time to listen to her. Please pray for more opportunities for those coming out of prison to be listened to and ask God to give you more opportunities to listen to those around you.

Chapter 4
From The Shop To The Train Station

Relaxed

With a can of cider in one hand and a cigarette in the other, balancing her black bag over her shoulder, a released woman can become a little more relaxed about chatting to me. I often start up a conversation with her when she comes out of the shop. I don't tend to go in because I don't want to be seen as condoning the buying of alcohol or cigarettes, or making her feel uncomfortable when she does; I appreciate the women have free choice. Now with their first objective completed, the released woman or women are more likely to engage. It is very often at this point that I begin to carry the woman's heavy bag. With their hands full the women are more likely to accept the offer and happier to begin to chat.

Small talk

As we wander to the station I make 'small talk'. Topics may include asking where they are going, how long it might take, how long they have been in prison. We may cover issues relating to their family and their offence, although I wait for them to bring these up. Some people want to keep themselves to themselves and continue to refuse any assistance, while others are happy to share their whole life story. If I can, I always try to steer the conversation in a positive direction. Whilst I never collude with anyone or condone their actions, neither do I condemn or judge. Almost all the women know what is commonly thought of as good behaviour and what are deemed to be the healthy options, so I don't usually state the obvious. I will, however, show a level of understanding when a woman shares some of her struggles and disappointments.

Just as with Emmy in chapter 1, it is at this stage a woman may start to open up and share her 'story'. This often features accounts relating to homelessness, abuse which may have begun in childhood, physical and sexual assaults, rejection, abandonment, addiction and criminality. It is amazing what someone can share in ten minutes if they want to and when there are just the two of you around. Towards the end of this stage in the journey she may talk more about her children – where they are and how old they are. They talk about their parents or partner and about what they hope to do that evening. Sadly, of course, some don't know where they will be that night.

A bed for the night

When we think of someone having a bed for the night, some of us picture it within the context of being comfortable that evening. For some people it just means being 'safe'. Drinking alcohol to the point where the person is no longer in control of their actions may appear to be unsafe and unwise, and onlookers may criticise the released women for spending some of their discharge grant in this way. Those commentators often throw out glib remarks like: 'Well, the grant won't go very far if they spent it on alcohol.' As if just over £46 was ever going to go very far, I want to say and occasionally do: *'Get real! If you knew that tonight the only guaranteed place you were going to "sleep" was in a drugs den or with your abusive partner and where you knew you were going to be forced to perform sexual acts or be raped and punched because there was nowhere else for you to go, wouldn't you want to get drunk first?'* It's either that or she stays out on the street where a complete stranger can rape her, steal from her and physically mess her up! My response may appear a little harsh but you want to hear the condescension in some people's voices as they slam the woman for the way she spends the money. A woman who gets drunk before she gets on the train possibly wants to celebrate her release in 'traditional' party style or maybe she is alcohol dependent due to her history or maybe it's because she knows what is coming next, and maybe it's for all three reasons! I'm not going to judge.

Shelter

When the subject of accommodation comes up it is clear that many people being released don't have anywhere safe for them to go. Councils and local authorities are under an obligation to accommodate the most vulnerable in society but, even so, the obligation is usually only to people with a connection to the area, having lived there in the past for some time or having been educated there, etc. However, if a person has defaulted on payment or contract with the authority in relation to housing, then the authority may in some cases no longer have a duty of care. Many people leaving prison without accommodation fall into this category. Whilst housing rules may change and more homeless people are registered with authorities, this does not mean more places are available or offered.

It is fair to say that some people lead extremely chaotic lifestyles and cannot reside successfully without complications surrounding them. This is a hugely complex subject and I am no expert. However, I'm aware there are no simple solutions for some people and authorities. All I know is that every week I walk to the station with someone who is of no fixed abode (NFA). They have no 'home' of their own to go to, no Bed & Breakfast accommodation to lodge at and no night shelter they can access. Theirs, if they are lucky, is a sofa to sleep on at a friend's place or, if they are not so lucky, their pimp's or a punter's bed and out the next day to 'earn' their bed for the next night. Michelle, a woman I have walked to the station in the past has told me, *'It hurts to be nowhere.'* Very often a homeless person doesn't want to talk too much about the reality of their situation as they walk down the road. After all, they are going to be living it soon enough.

Two churches

Halfway along the journey to the station there are two churches. One is a Salvation Army citadel and is usually open by the time we come past. Sometimes we have stopped off there for the woman to use the toilet, or popped in to see if they have a coat, especially if she didn't want to engage with me at the beginning of the journey. The staff are very helpful and, if needed, have made us a drink in the past. Currently they store a few emergency bags for homeless people which include toiletries, wet-wipes and personal hygiene products, underwear and socks, snack food, a flask, a torch, notebook, pen and Bible. This pack is donated by a local Christian charity. This Salvation Army has their own food bank and will donate food items from their store. They also have a supply of sleeping bags which the women can request if they need them. However, I have known some street homeless women turn down the offer of a bag as they say it is more dangerous to be wrapped up in a bag on the street than being covered with coats, as it is easier to get up and run if being attacked. If they are in a sleeping bag they can be restrained very easily.

Around this point in the journey I may suggest that if a woman is homeless she finds a local church in her area that may be able to support her with food or even clothing. It is encouraging to hear from the women of the various churches known to them that do run foodbanks or provide weekly meals or offer a shower and clean clothing; some churches even run night shelters, especially in the winter.

The second church is an Anglican church and equally as receptive but at present not always open when we walk by. They, too, have a real heart for the women being released and on occasions we have gone in there just to sit for a while, the woman quietly gathering her thoughts. During the last advent season the church was open in the mornings and we were encouraged to write prayer requests on a star to place on the Christmas tree at the front of the church; a couple of women did this. Outside the church they had an art installation in the form of a wooden shelter made to look like the type of shelter built for refugees who may be fleeing war or famine. On the backdrop was a picture of a family fleeing together – parents with a small child. This reflected the Christmas story of Mary and Joseph and the manger as well as the young family fleeing to Egypt when it became unsafe to stay in Israel. I placed in the bottom of the installation a sleeping bag tucked away in a black holdall, a blanket and a bottle of water for anyone who wanted to take them; the sleeping bag was eventually taken. I also encouraged the women as they walked by to write their names on the wooden walls, especially if they were going to be 'sofa-surfing' or street homeless at Christmas. I said they would be prayed for by name. Many took up this invitation. This was a powerful statement, telling the women they weren't forgotten and reminding the community of their plight and drawing attention to the nativity. Both churches are involved in the prison in different ways and such an encouragement to us.

Somewhere during this stage of the journey, the woman may comment on my role as a chaplain and ask why I do this particular work. I share that I believe it is the role of the chaplaincy to support where we can and that I know this can help the women being released, especially if no one is meeting them. I share that I believe this is what God would want us to do and it can be seen as his love in action, even if the woman has no faith. If this is the case, then I say very little about God as my main concern is to support the woman and definitely not preach to her. I believe sometimes actions speak louder than words. Yet there are times when the woman really wants to talk about God and perhaps ask questions. If this is the case then I will answer as best I can but sometimes there just isn't enough time.

Conversation time

There are so many different challenges to walking with the women and I never quite know how things are going to develop. I think it's that spontaneity that I thrive on and the uncertainty of how the conversation is going to proceed which keeps me alert. Some women engage in conversation with me out of politeness, whilst others have done away with politeness a long time ago! Some women just like to shock you. I was walking to the station with two women on one occasion and they were discussing how little money they had on them. One of them said she was going to 'work' as soon as she got back – she was a 'working girl' and was going to find some 'punters' for whom she could perform sexual favours. Then all of a sudden she turned to me and asked, 'How about it, sir, can I do anything for you?' The other woman, quite taken aback, reminded her that I was from the church. Her reply was, 'Well you won't be my first.' I just looked at her from over my glasses, no reply was required.

My approach to journeying with the women, and in particular to the conversations we may have, is to try and relate on the level the other person is at. Sometimes I drop in a little slang or vulgar language, describing life for some people as presenting as 'pants' (English/local slang for 'bad' or 'rubbish'). Again, this might appear a little aggressive or even unnecessary but me being blunt and straight to the point can help some people relate to me. I'm a white, male, middle-aged chaplain who, on the face of things, can appear to live a life quite remote from those women just coming out of prison, so anything that helps me connect I use. However, there is naturally some language I won't use. The Apostle Paul's comments in 1 Corinthians 9:22 are encouraging to me: *'To the weak I became weak, to win the weak. I have become all things to all people so that by all possible means I might save some.'* This is, of course, the reason why I wear the clothes I do: jeans and trainers as described earlier, although I have also been known to wear Hawaiian- or Polynesian-style short-sleeve shirts in the warmer months, reflecting my birthplace – brightly coloured and very noticeable. Not only can these be a talking point but also act as a distraction, which if someone is angry or nervous can be useful.

As we walk along together I try and drop in a few open questions, encouraging the woman to give more than a one-word answer. I've learnt not to predict the response. If the conversation appears to be going well I may ask a question relating to any children or grandchildren she may have. The replies can be very challenging as some women will share with great sadness how their children have been removed from them or even died shortly after birth due to being born with physical complications or died in an accident. I've been surprised a few times when a woman has said her son or daughter is in their early 30s and she only looks in her mid-40s. Of course there are some women who are in their 40s and look like they're in their late 50s. I have come across a lot of women who have had children when they themselves were in their mid-teens. Naturally some women don't want to talk to me about their family; it's usually clear from their first response. Some responses to my questions can be quite aggressive or blunt and some people don't hold back from letting me know what they really think about prison, their probation officer, the council regarding housing, social services, or perhaps their family!

Marcia

Not long ago I had an amazing conversation with a woman I'll call 'Marcia'. My engagement with her didn't start too well. Inside the prison she was loud and a little confrontational. The other women kept a distance from her. When we were outside my heart sank when she said she would like me to support her in walking to the station. Marcia was as loud outside as she was inside and couldn't help adding some colourful words to her conversation. As we began to walk down the drive I decided not to try to do anything but listen to her; she had a lot to say. By the time we passed the shop she started to slow down a little but her language was still splattered with swear words. Then suddenly she apologised for swearing and noted that she shouldn't do it in front of a chaplain. It was nothing I hadn't heard many times before but I thanked her for trying to refrain. She then went on to say that as a child she had gone to church and then she shared that she is a Christian and still prays. That wasn't the end of it; she then deduced that perhaps God had allowed her to come to prison as she was, in her words, 'out of control'. We then talked about God at a much deeper level, reflecting on what God may have in store for her. Her language was now more consistent with that of a Pentecostal preacher than what I had heard previously, with lots of 'praise the Lord' and 'Amen', replacing the swear words. By the time we got to the station I had heard about her mother and children, the work she used to do and her current lifestyle. At the station, Marcia asked me to pray for her, for healing and a miracle to happen. I waved a very different Marcia off at the station to the one I had first met in the holding cell.

Chatting faith

I have had several conversations regarding faith with the women I have walked alongside. Some state they have no faith, while others share traditional faith views regarding Islam, Christianity and Buddhism. I've had the same woman on two different occasions tell me about her belief system which involves calendars, numbers, horoscopes and I even think alien forces were mentioned. No seriously – they were! Sadly I can't remember her name or what she looks like so, who knows, I might be having this conversation again sometime. Horoscopes get mentioned quite a lot but not aliens – you'd think I'd remember her name!

Deeper conversations

Sometimes when I have journeyed with a woman before, we pick up the conversation from where we left off and she may say, 'You remember last time when I told you . . .' She may go on to tell me that she didn't get to where she told me she was heading – 'I'm straight to the probation office, then I'm going home . . .' She never made her appointment or home. I often give a wry smile and tell her I didn't think she would. She then shares how she wasn't ready to change and isn't ready now. I value the honesty as it takes the conversation to a different level. Quite often it's the women who have been in and out of prison who are the first to accept my offer of support. Even today as I write this, I had one woman who I know say to me, 'You are walking with me to the station, aren't you?' I've had a few women remind me of the first time we met and how she went off with the other women, not waiting for me, but now she appreciates our chat and the company.

Di

I can't quite remember how many times I've walked 'through the gate' with Di (again, not her real name); possibly four or five times. The first time she barely acknowledged me. She had family waiting in a car for her so she didn't need anything from me. Second time she acknowledged we'd met before but, as the previous time, she thought she had a lift waiting for her, although she wasn't a hundred per cent sure as she'd fallen out with the driver shortly after she was released previously. We did have a pleasant conversation prior to her release, during which time she told me she had a significant drink problem, estranged relationships with family members and that she was her own worst enemy at times. On the third occasion she confirmed she had no one meeting her and she was walking to the station. However, it was clear she was still on 'self-destruct' and didn't need me to assist her as there were things she wanted to do alongside some of the others being released that day – getting drunk was one of them. On the fourth occasion we had a long, open conversation where she admitted she had a serious drug addiction as well as an alcohol one. She agreed to me walking her to the station and on the way she didn't buy any alcohol. However, there is likely to be a fifth time as she is in prison at the time of me writing this. Of course she may get transferred to another prison or be released on a day I'm not working. I believe she is normally arrested for failure to comply with her licence conditions, which include remaining sober in public – one requirement she finds hard to keep. The last time I waved her off, however, she was sober! I like to think that with every engagement there is a better chance of a successful outcome.

Deeper still

Going deeper brings other opportunities. As the woman begins to trust me she may share some deeply personal things such as when she was raped and by whom, or some of the horrible things she has done in the past. Again, I'm not there to judge but rather listen as she wants to open up her heart a little. There are some people who will open up their heart to just about anybody – serial open-uppers. I may have heard the story before or overheard it being told to someone else while they were waiting to be released. Sometimes the story changes slightly. Sometimes she asks for my opinion. I have to be careful because I don't want her quoting or misquoting me saying, 'And the chaplain agrees with me,' when all I did was nod along to the story.

Now there are times when I find myself saying, 'Why?' It might be because I want a bit more background information but then again it might be in the context of 'So why did you do it . . . say it . . . go there?' If I know the woman well I might even say it as a challenge: 'But you already knew what was going to happen, so why did you end up there?' Often the woman will agree it wasn't the best idea she'd had. Sometimes we'll be able to discuss it and I ask her what she'll do next time. Sadly, I've had some tell me they'd do the same again, and then describe themselves as 'stupid' and sometimes it's hard to disagree. Yet to be fair to them, some of the options they have leave them with little choice. Some of the women will challenge themselves without me having to say anything, and come up with how they would like to do things differently next time.

Reflection

Luke 24:25-27

*He said to them, 'How foolish you are, and how slow
to believe all that the prophets have spoken! Did not
the Messiah have to suffer these things and then enter
his glory?' And beginning with Moses and all the
Prophets, he explained to them what was said in all
the Scriptures concerning himself.*

How foolish

I love the way Jesus firstly listens to the confused travellers then
has a little go at them: 'How foolish you are.' He's heard them
give a clear account of all that had recently happened, including
the good news of the resurrection, and yet they are unwilling
to believe or even hang around to see if it's true. By the time he
admonishes them he's earnt the opportunity. He has engaged
with them on their terms, walking alongside them. He has shown
interest in their situation and listened to their story. Now it is his
time to interject and he doesn't hold back. In Jesus' opinion the
two of them needed to be challenged and educated. It appears
that he not only went into some detail but presented it in a way
they could understand.

As a former Probation Service Officer I can't help but
occasionally challenge those I walk with. Sometimes it's with
a knowing look – such as peering over my glasses, or with my
mouth wide open and arms stretched out – a look of exasperation

as much as to say, 'Did you really say that?' without actually me saying anything. On other occasions I might say, 'What!' or 'Why?' I've been known to challenge the women by saying that they knew what was going to happen to them, what the outcome was likely to be. But I like it best when they admonish themselves, when they reflect on how silly they were not to listen to their own wise counsel – the small inner voice challenging them to do things differently and yet once again ignored.

There have been plenty of times when I wished I had listened to my own inner voice. Especially late at night when I hear myself reason why I shouldn't go to bed and rather stay up and watch some mindless television. Yet as I do this I am also aware I'm often grumpy when I haven't had enough sleep. And guess what? If 'Mr Grumpy' doesn't possess me in the morning he is certainly there in the evening! I admonish myself and get to bed earlier. But sadly the damage is done and I've been grumpy with those around me. When tired I can become a little irrational and perhaps read too much into things; a throwaway comment aimed in my direction can devastate me or I can issue the comment with the same effect upon an unsuspecting victim. It's at this point I need someone to highlight how 'foolish' I've been. Thankfully I have people in my life who will challenge me.

Questions

1. Name at least one 'foolish' thing you are prone to do?
2. Who is the person you allow to challenge you when your 'foolishness' gets the better of you?
3. How do you feel when they highlight your weakness?

4. Is there anyone in your network of family and friends who you have 'earnt' the right to challenge?

For prayer

Please pray those people leaving prison will have the strength and wisdom to listen to their inner voice or the voice of a trusted person, one which is challenging them to do what they believe is right and healthy. Pray also that if you don't already have someone who can challenge you when you are tempted to think or do the 'foolish' things in your life, that you will find someone who can highlight how 'foolish' you are in the same insightful way that Jesus did with the two on the way to Emmaus.

Chapter 5
At The Train Station

Slowing down

The nearer to the station, the slower the pace becomes. It's not a particularly long walk but if all the walking the woman has done for several months is two to three minutes at a time – walking from the prison house block to the workshop area – then these ten or fifteen minutes can be exhausting. I always try to keep the conversation flowing and this is when I really try to encourage the woman. We look at the positives in her life, having on occasions talked about the negatives. Sometimes the positives are her children and it's good to talk about them. I often hear how they have made a success of their lives, have good jobs and still make the effort to stay in touch with their mum. It's great to hear a proud mum talk about her children. It still brings a smile to my face when a woman tells me that her child is studying law at university – could be useful in the future; you may be surprised at how many times over the years I've heard this.

We have been known to discuss our skills, focusing on her specific strengths. Several of the women I've walked along with have had a gift for poetry or drawing, the other day a woman recited a 'rap' composition she had created. I'm not known for my love of rap music but I certainly appreciated the effort and creativity she had put into the verse. I was also humbled by the fact that she wanted to share it with me – but don't ask me to recite it! However, having said that I'm not known for my love of rap music, I can certainly recommend a couple of tracks by

Guvna B – a rap/grime artist. I love his version of 'Nothing But the Blood' featuring Deitrick Haddon – the video with the white balloons is great – and I also like 'Everyday', the official video is powerful!

Sometimes a woman will talk about her belief system and how her faith has helped her to cope with everything she has been through and how she is going to re-engage with it when she's resettled. We discuss things that can motivate her and it is here that I try to build up her self-esteem. I highlight something positive I have noticed on the journey, such as her personality, for example, her hope that one day all will work out well for her or work out well for her children, especially if she is estranged from them; or maybe I compliment her on her resilience – she keeps going whatever comes her way. I know that in a few minutes' time the excitement of getting on the train will take over and her focus will shift.

Around the corner

By the time we turn the last corner and spot the station only a hundred metres away, the woman can't wait to get there and get on with her journey and life, whatever it holds. In that last minute the woman speeds up again and, almost without thought for anyone or any traffic, she heads straight to the building; her excitement can be palpable.

As we near the station I remind the woman to get her travel warrant ready as she needs to exchange it for a valid ticket. Often there is panic as the woman searches for the crumpled piece of paper: which pocket did she put it in or is it in her bag or in her bra? With a sigh of relief, she finds it and strides even more quickly to the door. I have to exercise wisdom when a woman is searching for her warrant, knowing when to look away when she goes up top to retrieve it – once again I can't help smiling when I look at the faces of the onlookers who are wondering what she is doing.

For many women in prison, and probably in the community too, the bra can be one of the safest places to store things; very much a no-go area, when a woman rummages there it is certainly time to look away! If the woman is scrambling around in her bag or bags to see if it is tucked away in something, it can be tempting to dive in and help her. Caution is required here also as I never know what I may come across in there and it could be a little embarrassing for both of us: her 'working' underwear is something I really don't need to see. As she's just come out of prison I hope there shouldn't be any drugs paraphernalia in there but you never know, especially pipes and needles. I always ask first before I assist in the process. If there is a queue forming at the ticket office then speeding up the process can be useful as she looks again in every pocket of her jeans and coat; searches deep within her handbag, turfs out the contents of the two or more bags full of belongings and delves once more into her bra. This activity can take place anywhere from the prison to the station but is more frantic when they are within sight of the station.

As well as looking for her travel warrant the woman may also check what money she has on her as the corner is turned. This is because there is another shop to tempt her. Cigarettes and vape cartridges are often bought here. Some women will ask at this point if there is a cash machine nearby so they can check if their benefits are still being paid in to their account or if her boyfriend has deposited the money he promised her.

One-way ticket

All tickets issued via the warrant are single fares, one-way destinations. A very few women will come back to the station on a return visit. These are those who return to see their 'friends', the women they promised to keep in touch with, whom they promised to visit. But the majority who return to the prison do so in a prison van.

For those who have left prison alone, their journey to the station is a very different one from the journey made by the 'girls' – the gang who come out at the same time. When I escort the lone person, the conversation is very different from that of the gang, who are often loud and abrasive in their manner. The sole traveller is usually quieter and more engaged. At the ticket office she politely hands over her warrant. I always stand next to the woman just in case she doesn't understand what the ticket officer says. Sometimes the woman is unsure of the route she needs to take, so we ask for a printout. When the ticket has been purchased, we either stop a short while in the waiting room or perhaps go for a coffee nearby. If the train is about to arrive, I walk with the woman to the correct platform, reminding her which station she is heading for or where she needs to change. If all goes well, we exchange a wave as the train pulls away with her heading safely out of town.

If only it was that simple! Sometimes the ticket office is closed. This can send the woman into a spin and worry her, particularly if she has vowed never to break the law again. I reassure her that all she needs to do is board the train and if there is a guard on board show them the warrant and explain that this office was closed. They'll either issue a ticket or suggest she gets it changed at the station she gets off at, especially if she transferring to another line. There are, however, many women who are experienced at this process and just don't bother at getting the warrant changed. In truth some of the women I journey to the station with don't mind if they get caught travelling the rails without a ticket or travel warrant, because the worst that can happen is that they get arrested and within a day or two are back in the safety of the prison, which is in fact the best thing they believe can happen to them.

'Girls' on stage

Life at the station can get a little more challenging when the 'girls' arrive – multiple women descending at once. The decibels go up, as do the risks. They encourage each other and often it is to get up to mischief. They can be rude, especially towards the ticket officer, who sometimes has to put up with a lot of unwanted behaviour. My standing alongside the women can reduce this. It is not uncommon for the released women to speak deliberately loud enough so everyone in the waiting room can hear them, boasting that they have just come out of prison, as if everyone there didn't already know that fact given the bags they are carrying. Recently, as they waited in the queue to exchange their warrants, two of them discussed, loud enough so the teenage girls waiting for the train to arrive could hear, how easy it is to 'pay' for sex from the other prisoners and how 'easy' they are. I, of course, put a stop to that conversation pretty quickly!

They also encourage one another to steal, for instance from the café near the station. One day a woman stole the tips money and was spotted by a customer. The shop worker got the money back. I remember on another occasion in the waiting area by the ticket office a couple of women changed into nicer outfits in front of onlookers and then said to an onlooker, 'That's it, have a good look.' It is as if they are on stage and playing up to the audience. And naturally they can't resist interacting with their captive audience – 'Have you got a smoke?' they will ask some unsuspecting bystander. I guess this is better than being asked if anyone would like to pay for sex as they need a little money!

Hanging around

If the woman thinks she has time then she may use the station's only women's toilet – one cubicle. There have been a few times when a couple of the women have gone in together, apparently to do their make-up. Sadly, I think they may also have taken drugs together behind the safety of the locked door. I have had to knock on the door to tell them to hurry up as either the train is coming or there is a queue forming. I am also aware that on the odd occasion a woman has 'used' – taken drugs on her way to the station or even just outside. These have been supplied by the boyfriend who came to meet her and, true to his word, 'brought her a little present'. There are also drug dealers who hang around on the off chance that they can be of service. My presence can sometimes act as deterrence, particularly for the woman.

Leanne and Kirsty

I walked, as I often do, with two women who were well known to the prison. They, like so many, talked about wanting to resist the temptation to take drugs again. However, I suspected they had declared this before but sadly not managed to stick to their hope. We walked to the station, me carrying one of their bags. Unfortunately we had quite a wait till their train came in. I bought them a coffee at the café next to the station and they sat outside while they waited for me to purchase it and bring it out to them. While I queued inside I saw a man approach them. Leanne looked at me through the window and back at the chap. I couldn't hear what was said but I knew the gist of the conversation. He was offering them drugs but they declined, I could see clearly no exchange took place. As soon as I came out with their drinks they told me what happened and how they had refused his offer. I was so proud of them and told them so.

A few weeks later a wonderful nun who has a ministry in caring for street workers and visits the prison regularly, told me that she had met up with Leanne recently and how Leanne told her about the incident at the station. Apparently, because I was there only a few feet away getting the coffee, this gave her the courage to say no to the dealer. Just my presence had made a significant difference on that occasion.

For women with an alcohol dependency, waiting around for the train can also be a major challenge as they can find themselves

wandering back to the shop on the corner to stock up on whatever their preference is: cans or bottles or both.

Dee

Dee had a problem with both drug misuse and alcohol dependency. When she was released she didn't have any reporting instructions as she had served her whole sentence. As a result Dee wasn't in a hurry to get home to her family. She had stopped at the off-licence and was 'downing' a can of the strong stuff. I don't know how many cans she had in her bag but I guessed she had at least a couple more tucked away. We walked to the station; I assisted her in getting the ticket and talked through the route she needed to take – changing twice before reaching her final destination.

As Dee was in no hurry she left the station for a smoke and another can. She missed her train but that didn't bother her. Then someone on a bike rode up to us and asked if we knew where there was a working pay phone as the two by the station were broken. We couldn't help but the person hung around and wanted to complain about how little support there was for people struggling on benefits. Dee sensed there was more to the person and thought they used drugs, so asked them if they had any dealers' numbers. Funnily enough, the person on the bike believed they could help and, although their mobile phone was out of credit, they did have a number saved that could assist Dee. But Dee looked at me and then said to the person not to bother. However, a third can was now opened and Dee was becoming slightly worse for wear. Unfortunately, I had booked an appointment with a colleague and I needed to get back to the prison, leaving Dee alone to get on the next train herself and wishing her all the best. Luckily my meeting was cut short so after twenty-five minutes I returned to the station hoping not to find Dee. But there she was, in exactly the same spot and drunk.

I persuaded Dee to come with me for a coffee, which she did. After a good long chat and a strong coffee, she sobered up a little. Dee felt she had very little going for her: she was an alcoholic, had to go back and live with her mum, and had no money and not a lot to look forward to. After a good chat about how lovely her mum was, even though her mum had many problems, Dee talked herself into focusing her mind on getting the next train. In her semi-drunk state Dee was wobbly on the platform so I kept her away from the edge. When the train pulled in, I helped her onto it and waved her off. She thanked me for my time and for listening to her. She left with a smile on her face and landed a hug on me too! I'm glad I was there to stop her from falling onto the tracks and get her safely on the train.

On and off the platform

Not everyone is safe alone on the platform though. One day I was walking with two released women, one of whom had an escort from a support organisation. The other was presenting as uncoordinated the moment she walked out of the gate and the alcohol she purchased on the way did not add any stability to the situation. When we got to the Salvation Army I popped in for a coat for her, and knowing I was going to be delayed a few minutes we agreed they should walk on to the station. When I arrived at the platform I could only spot the woman with the escort. As

I got nearer to them I saw the head and shoulders of the other woman appear from over the edge of the platform – trackside. Then a leg appeared but she couldn't raise it high enough to get any purchase. She was definitely struggling and it appeared no one was doing anything about it. Of course I rushed over to the edge and pulled her up onto the platform. In her last attempt to rescue herself she stood on the rail but she was still too low. Had she moved further back she could have touched the live rail and that would have certainly been 'goodbye'. As it was, three minutes after my assistance the train came; she'd never have made it out of there without someone coming to her aid.

On at least two occasions I've had to split up a couple of the women on the platform as they were close to fighting each other. One accused the other of stealing something from her, and on a separate occasion one of the women was saying something derogatory about the other one.

One hot summer's morning two women decided to change their clothes into something cooler, which was understandable. What was not understandable was why they chose to do it on the platform in front of dozens of commuters. One took off her jogging bottoms and put on knee length trousers while the other one took off her sweat shirt and put on a T-shirt; both revealing their underwear. There was a woman on the platform who I knew and she talked to the women as they changed, I couldn't look at them! As soon as they began I told them to change in the toilet but that was too far for them to go, just the other side of the station.

Sadly, on one occasion I was waiting with some women who were minding their own business when a couple of teenage lads started to throw insults at them. For a short while it was very unpleasant. The women can get all sorts of reactions from the public. Some people ignore them, while others just stare. Some people make you feel like scum as they walk by, they pull a most disapproving look. I know this because I've been at the end of their gaze when I've been dressed in my hoody, jeans and trainers whilst carrying a woman's bag. There's an assumption I'm with them and they are right, I am. However, some onlookers on the platform present as reassured when I occupy the women and distract them from engaging with the other passengers, some of whom also look terrified, especially when in close proximity to those who are very excited to be 'out'!

Keesh

A volunteer and I had walked with Keesh down to the station. Keesh did most of the talking, mainly about life in prison, nothing too detailed or heavy. Not 'heavy' for those of us who work in prisons but for this particular volunteer it was still all new, so she was a little challenged.

When we got to the platform we had several minutes to wait. I led us down towards the end of the platform, sensing that she was going to be loud and somewhat opinionated, so I thought it best to keep away from other commuters. When we got to a metal bench she climbed up onto the back rest, placing her feet on the seat. She stated she has OCD – Obsessive-Compulsive Disorder – and as a result was paranoid about cleanliness and had a fear of sitting on something dirty. A little ironic as she was making the seat dirty for the next person. However, it was at this stage that she began to share deep issues in her life, including trauma in the past. She also disclosed her offence – I'm so glad I didn't wind her up about dirty shoes on seats, she might have shown us a side to her we hadn't previously experienced. We stood by the bench as she told us her story. I make it a point of keeping as good eye contact as possible with the women, so as she was perched on the back of the seat and we were standing we were at about the same head height. There are times when I will deliberately sit when a woman is standing, giving her a dominant position; some women are unfamiliar with this as most of the men in 'her' life dominate her.

This became a special time with Keesh as she opened up and we listened to her brokenness. Somewhere in her story was a moment when as a child she went to Sunday school and even as an adult had a Christian faith. It felt natural to pray for her on the platform, there and then; and it was obvious in her response that she appreciated it. As we parted she grabbed both of us in a hug and waved goodbye.

Quality time

In the one mile from the holding cell to the platform I know the woman is weighing me up, thinking, 'Can he be trusted if I open up? What will he do with the information if I share it with him? What will he think of me and can he handle it?' When the woman is assured that I'm trustworthy she may disclose things, especially when all the business is done – her ticket, cigarettes and drink (alcoholic or soft) are purchased and we are now waiting for the train. Although we may not have a long time to wait it can still be a time of quality and importance. I know how much some women value the opportunity to just unload, without any judgement or intervention, just to have space to speak some things out loud without any comment or opinion offered. Some women just want to be listened to, not because they want me to give them the solution to their problems but so they can explore their options, however limited they may be.

This is where respect really kicks in and it starts with me. When I give the woman respect and value her as I know God values her, her response is very often to show her appreciation.

Tina and Al

When I first met Tina she was in the holding cell with two others. One woman had a through-the-gate worker meeting her outside at the gate and the other woman was presenting as very keen to keep herself to herself, refusing my offer to walk with her to the station. In the end she got a bus from the top of the drive to the station – two stops.

Tina was very engaging and shared how she had enjoyed attending the Sunday-morning services in the prison, many of the women do as they can be lively events with lots of singing and a little dancing too. However, Tina stated she didn't need my help as her boyfriend Al was going to meet her, and she was hoping he would be bringing her a 'present'. She shared that she had an issue with drugs and therefore I presumed the present would be of that nature.

When the gate went back the woman with the through-the-gate worker went off with her, the other woman headed down the drive and Al was there to meet Tina. He was in the visitors' car park so I presumed he'd come by car. As I wasn't required and it was raining I went into the prison's Community Coffee Shop. However, while I was there I began to think that perhaps I ought to go to the station and just make sure the woman catching the bus got on the train. As I wasn't with anyone else I drove down to the station, not wanting to get too wet. I couldn't find anywhere to park so I went back to the Anglican church, parked up there and walked the short distance to the station. By the time I got there a train was pulling out and no one was left on the platform, so I walked back to my car.

As I approached the church I noticed someone leaning on the wall of the car park: it was Tina. She was using her phone to try and get hold of a minicab. It turned out that Al had come by train and was at the back of the car park on his phone. I explained that there was a minicab firm right by the station which was only a few minutes' walk away, so the three of us went to the station.

Tina introduced me to Al as the chaplain she had told him about as they walked down the road. Almost immediately she began to talk to me about church, her own faith and quiz me about my mine. She wanted to know what Pentecostals believe in and how different that might be to how she was brought up. I'm always careful not to say negative things about other denominations or theologies, and always quick to highlight the merits in all traditions. She was already quite knowledgeable and wanted to know more of the things of the Holy Spirit. As we approached the station it was clear Tina had much more she wanted to ask and know about and poor old Al was going to have to suffer while she got her 'fix' of faith and information.

We went into the coffee shop by the station and, after ordering a drink each, we sat down to talk some more. The conversation just got deeper and deeper. She wanted to know about the power and influence of the Holy Spirit and professed to want to have a radical change in her life, one where Jesus was central. I think Al had heard some of this before and was happy to let her carry on chatting while he made phone calls and sent texts. After deliberately missing one train she was keen for me to pray with her. As we had covered many topics including theology, her life history and current situation, there was a lot to pray about; this was not a short prayer. We also prayed for Al and she affirmed her belief and commitment to God. As Al walked back into the shop, Tina told him what we had being doing and then got up and said she was going to the shop nearby. This left me talking to Al and the barista who had seen me pray in the shop on several occasions in the past.

Tina was gone a long while and I was just about to go looking for her when she reappeared with a card. It was for me. On the front of the card was a picture of a coloured sheep surrounded by other plain sheep and words saying, 'Thanks . . . Ewe are one in a million.' She had written inside:

Dear Simian (I have been called all sorts of things over the years with many different spellings)

Thank You So Much

I thought this card very fitting as you have just found the newest member of your flock (you being the colour that you have just breathed into my life) thank you for being the first big thing to happen to me on a day where by you touched my heart and soul when I needed it most thank you much love Tina.

As you can imagine I was surprised and a little taken aback. Plenty of people thank me for what I do but this was going a little bit further. The next day I took the card into the chaplaincy team where I left it.

I waved Tina and Al off knowing that for a few minutes we'd had some quality time together and went back to my car with renewed vigour and oblivious to the rain.

Reflection

Luke 24:28-29

As they approached the village to which they were going, Jesus continued on as if he were going further. But they urged him strongly, 'Stay with us, for it is nearly evening; the day is almost over.' So he went in to stay with them.

Trust

By the time the two got to the village it was clear there had been a real connection between them and Jesus, even though they still hadn't appreciated that it was really him they had spent so much time with. This connection had developed throughout their journey and began with Jesus greeting them and asking what was on their mind. The rapport deepened as he listened to them and then gave his thoughts. By the time they had reached their destination, Jesus was now treated like a friend. A real bond had developed, and their trust in him was evident as they asked him to stay with them. Trust can take a while to develop and needs to be earnt. Sometimes it can take years to grow and often it is through mutual sharing. It can take courage to step out and share personal issues, especially if you are not too sure how the other person will receive the information you're disclosing. Jesus was in their minds no longer an ignorant traveller unaware of recent events but someone who really understood what was bothering the two as they walked together. I don't think it was out of politeness that the two invited Jesus to stay with them; they valued him.

I always feel privileged when a woman opens up her heart and shares personal information with me. I feel trusted and valued, even if I'm aware she has said the same thing to other people or even if it appears unbelievable. In fact we all have worries and issues that can at times 'lay us low', confuse us or even leave us mentally paralysed. Whilst I am in a much stronger and safer place concerning my dyslexia, it can still emotionally trip me up at times. I am extremely grateful to those I have unloaded my frustration and occasional pain to. My wife Julie has heard much of this over the years, as have a few close friends. Pastor Desmond, who heads up the church I attend, is also someone I have trusted with my pain, especially when it comes to form filling. Anyone in the UK who works in any capacity with vulnerable people will be familiar with needing to complete a Disclosure and Barring Service (DBS) check. These days the forms that need to be completed by the applicant are online. I 'stress out' when I have to complete any form online. As a result I click the wrong buttons, enter data in the wrong place and as I'm so paranoid I quadruple check what I have entered, therefore taking at least twice as long as those competent in this area. Pastor Desmond and I have journeyed together over several years now, so I feel comfortable in allowing him to see my utter meltdown at even the thought of having to go through this process. I trust him not to judge me but rather understand what I'm experiencing emotionally – the fear and anxiety that grips me. It is one thing to hear about it from me and quite another to see me in complete panic!

Jesus listened to the pain of the two on the road, he listens to my pain and I'm sure has heard your pain too. 'They' trusted him; I trust him as well as trusting those he sends to journey with me in my time of need.

Questions

1. Can you think of something you struggle with and that you are embarrassed to share publicly?
2. Is there someone in your life who you trust enough to share it with?
3. Are you someone who others trust enough to share their secrets with?
4. Have you ever been in a situation when someone you didn't know ended up sharing their concerns and confusion with you? How did you respond?

For prayer

Please pray that the people being released from prison will have others around them they can trust and depend on. Pray also that if you don't have anyone in your life you can trust, God will bring such people across your path and pray that you, too, can be someone others will look to trust.

Chapter 6
On The Train

The goodbye

There have been times when I have walked someone to the station and it is painfully obvious that they have barely tolerated my company. Perhaps they accepted my offer in the hope that I'd buy them a packet of cigarettes or a can of their favourite beverage, only to be disappointed by my lack of engagement. By the time we get to the station they are very keen to part company and certainly don't want me waving them off, so I tend not to hang around waiting for the train and, if I do, then I do it from a distance, usually from the other platform or in the waiting room. However, the majority of the women are happy for me to see them off.

There is rarely a week goes by when I haven't ended up waving someone off after a shaky start. It is amazing that in under a mile someone can greet you very coldly and yet end up saying a very warm goodbye. This is when I know I've made a difference.

The 'goodbyes' come in different forms: from no physical contact and only a verbal acknowledgement that they are on their way, through to a handshake or even a bear-hug of a hearty goodbye followed by them attempting to land a kiss on my cheek – not something I encourage but sometimes it's almost unavoidable, although I do try my hardest to 'duck out' of them if I can. However, all the 'goodbyes' are caught on the station cameras and witnessed by the general public, so I know if anyone raised concern there is enough evidence to suggest I was the victim of their embrace, not that I'm formally complaining – it's a hazard of the job. After all, the way we say goodbye is always dictated by the woman leaving. If a woman keeps her distance I keep mine; if she holds out her hand then I offer mine, and if she puts her arms out to offer a hug then I may on rare occasions allow the embrace. This is her taking control and me responding politely.

I'm a firm believer in the theory that the way a person leaves can affect the way they arrive at their next destination. A friendly goodbye could mean that, should I meet them again a few months later, we can start from a positive position.

Fist bumping

These days I am known for my fist bumping, especially when saying goodbye on the platform. Fist bumping is similar to a handshake or a high five and can also imply mutual respect. It is when two people greet or acknowledge each other by bumping their closed fists together. I first started doing this when I was Managing Chaplain in the prison. There was one particular officer who encouraged me in this form of greeting and before long I was fist bumping the women as they left chapel at the end of church services instead of shaking hands. Of course, not everyone appreciated this form of greeting and, occasionally, I have been told to behave myself and shake formally. Most of the women I walk with to the station have no problems with me fist bumping them as a greeting and some have even been known to walk out of their way when we meet back in the prison – just to fist bump me. What it says is 'let's connect' and, when I am walking with someone to the train station out in the community, that is no bad thing. After a woman offers me her hand for a handshake goodbye, I may then offer my fist for a fist bump. This often brings a smile to her face and surely smiling as we say goodbye has to be a positive way to part.

As the train pulls in

During the 'goodbye' process I will often remind the woman once again of the particular station she is to get off at if she needs to change trains. I may wish her well for the future and say I hope she gets to her first appointment. To some I may just ask them to keep themselves safe, as we both know they are heading towards a challenging few days. If I've had a conversation with them regarding their faith, then I may encourage them to connect as soon as possible with their church, temple, mosque or synagogue. It is quite common for a woman to ask me to bless her or pray for her as the train is coming in. Often to their surprise I offer up a short prayer there and then. Some women are unfamiliar with travelling by train so I can even find myself pushing the button to open the door. If a woman has several bags with her then I will offer to put some of the bags on the train for her. Perhaps it isn't surprising that as the train arrives some women can have a look of fear on their faces, especially for those who don't like trains or travelling alone.

Doors closed

As the doors close behind the women most make their way to the nearest seat, yet some will want to walk through the carriage. I'm not sure if this is to escape those they've got on the train with or just to find a quiet space or a 'victim' to annoy. Many of the women will look out of the window as the train pulls away from the station and give me a wave. I often give a thumbs-up sign as well as a wave back, smile and mouth 'all the best' or 'good luck'. Some are too preoccupied with sorting out their bags to notice the train pulling away but I still wave just in case they look up.

Into the unknown

As the train pulls out of the station I can often find myself breathing a sigh of relief. Some journeys to the station can be exhausting and occasionally, when there are several women all having a chaotic nature about them, it can feel a little like herding cats as I try to support and direct them through the ticket process and onto the platform. They are naturally excited, nervous and distracted but usually well behaved. As I make my way out of the station I'm aware of a sense of relief that 'they are on the train' and off to . . .? Some I'm sure will get to their agreed destination but others I know won't make it. The truth is I never really know how it is going to turn out for them and I'm sure some of them have no idea either. I try not to ponder the unknown, but rather hope and pray it all goes according to the safest plan; after all, worrying about it isn't going to achieve anything.

Success

I often get asked if I worry about whether they make it to their destination. It can be said in the context of if they arrive safely it is deemed to be a success and if they fail to get to their appointments then they or I have failed. I measure success slightly differently. I'm successful if I have managed to engage with the woman, or if during the process of leaving the prison I have been helpful, perhaps having been able to direct her to the visitors' car park or the Community Coffee Shop if she is waiting for someone. If I'm journeying to the station with her then success is if I have supported the woman to avoid being tempted by alcohol or drugs, get to the station without losing anything or her taking something that doesn't belong to her, and then finally waving her off on the right train in a positive frame of mind – that is my definition of success.

In reality it's not as clear cut as it sounds. I guess there are varying degrees of 'success'. The woman may have bought a can of alcohol but still gets on the right train, or she accuses a fellow traveller from the prison of stealing something from her but still gets on the right train. The woman gets to the station without incident but then informs me she is going to get off the train a few stops earlier than her original destination.

Loz

I walked three women to the station. Loz had been talking to the others being released about using drugs as soon as possible. All three stopped at the Community Coffee Shop and got a hot drink. They packed and repacked their bags. Loz then mentioned to me that on previous occasions when released from prison she had arranged for someone to collect her and bring drugs with them. This time, however, she didn't organise this as she didn't want to be tempted, yet she is still talking about using. She also informed me she has had a problem with alcohol but wasn't going to buy any on the way to the station. As we walked towards the end of the drive, the other two talked about going into the shop and she said she'd wait outside. At the door she changed her mind and said she wanted to use the cash machine in the store. To get to this she had to walk past the shelves full of alcohol. She came out of the shop knowing she had significant funds in her account. One of the others asked if she had bought any 'drink'. She answered 'no', but then asked them if they wanted some as she had money. They both put in their order and she came back out of the shop with three cans.

On the way to the station all three drank their cans and bizarrely thanked me. They didn't mention what they are thanking me for just that they are thanking me. It was almost as if they thought I'd bought the alcohol – I think the 'drink' had already got to them. As we passed the Anglican church, Loz and one of the others opted to sign their names on the art installation.

Finally we got to the platform; two, including Loz, were on one platform while the third woman was on the opposite side heading in a direction away from London. The one travelling to London with Loz got friendly with another commuter who Loz and I suspected was going to deal her some drugs and she got on the slower train with him. Loz held back and waited for the right train. As Loz got on she thanked me once again, then off she went.

Was this a success? Loz succumbed to the temptation to buy and consume alcohol but didn't take the opportunity to get hold of drugs. From my point of view I thank God for the chance to support people like Loz and I most certainly see this journey to the station as a success. Yet I don't know whether she will carry on talking about wanting to 'use' later and eventually give in to the temptation. Perhaps she resisted going with the other woman on the slow train because I was there?

Lightbulbs

Maybe success could also be measured in 'lightbulb' moments, that moment when something clicks and makes sense, possibly for the first time. Tina (of Tina and Al) appeared to have had that when she wrote, *'Thank you for being the first big thing to happen to me on a day where by you touched my heart and soul when I needed it most thank you.'* She certainly got on the train a very different person to the one I met in the holding cell.

From the time the door closes I have no idea what happens. I have a friend who got on the same train as someone I was waving off, who told me later how the woman had shared her life story with her – in full colour and quite loudly – then after a while left my friend to share her story with someone else. I can't be sure but it sounds like the woman was presenting as if she could do with a bit of money from my friend and when it wasn't forthcoming moved on to someone else.

Whilst I could be a little concerned about the women as they travel together, it has been known for them to quieten down and collectively focus on the day ahead, so one woman told me. But, sadly, this is not necessarily the norm and the terrorising of those around them may continue.

Knowing that some of the women I support come back a short while later, a few people have asked me why I bother and what difference I make – what does it matter if I'm there or not there? When asked this question I reflect upon the starfish story.

The Starfish Story

You may already be familiar with the Starfish Story. You may wish to search for it online – there are many different versions and some are attributed to Loren Eiseley. Here is my version, one I have told to countless people over many years.

There was a man walking a dog along a beach. In the distance he saw another man at the water's edge – bending down, standing up, bending down, standing up. He was continually doing this. The man with the dog walked over to the other man and, as he got closer, he noticed hundreds and hundreds of starfish washed up along the beach. The man was picking them up and throwing them back into the water, hoping they would catch the outward current. The man with the dog asked what he was doing and the other man gave an obvious reply: 'I'm throwing them back.' The man with the dog looked at the vast number of starfish and what appeared to be a hopeless task, with so many to rescue, and said 'What does it matter, what difference does it make?' referring to the few that were being thrown back. The man replied, *'It makes a difference to this one,'* as he threw one back and again he said, *'it makes a difference to this one'*, as another was launched into the sea.

For over twenty years that has been my 'mantra'. I can't 'save' all of the people all of the time, but I can make a difference to a few.

One mile to make a difference

So often we limit ourselves. In prison we are forever saying we wish someone had got a longer sentence because we really feel that with a bit more time and support the person could turn things around.

With a sigh it is often said, *'What can you do in five minutes?'* But even in a short space of time you can make an impact. Smile at a complete stranger and often you'll get a smile back. Open a door for someone struggling and they are likely to say 'thank you'. Simple actions can get positive responses.

I know that a simple one-mile journey from the prison main gate to the local train station can have a huge impact. I'm not about cosmic changes, just making a small difference to someone's day. If that day starts well, it may continue to go well. If it goes well long enough, it might end well. If the first day has gone well, the next day may go well. If several days go well, a week may go well. If one week goes well, two weeks may go well. If two weeks go well, why not one month or two months or six months or . . . If the day starts badly it just might continue that way. If it starts well and gets worse at least you can look back and say, 'I had a good start.' And now you know what 'good' looks like, perhaps it can be replicated later on.

Many of us are familiar with the Chinese proverb, 'A journey of a thousand miles begins with one step.' And there are many other clichés but the principle is the same: just one step, just one action can make a difference. So, let's be positive difference makers!

Difference can also be measured by how a previous experience compares to a current one. Women often comment on how nice it is to have someone with them this time they are released. I have had a few say that if they had met me last time then perhaps they wouldn't have 'hit the bottle' straight away and may have got to their first appointment safely. In addition to the practical difference I can make, I also try to focus thoughts from fear to hope. I try to bring 'hope' into the conversation, always trying to look towards something positive. Hope is a great thing to hold on to if you can and much better than fear!

A time to reflect

On the train some women are alone again, having waved me goodbye. For many this is not a bad thing as they now have a little time to reflect on where they are going and what they have to do, perhaps even what hope there is for them. I'm sure some women read their licences again, repack their bags and try to ring people if they have credit or a sim card in their phone and the battery hasn't run down. I'm an optimist: the glass is always half full, the clouds will move away one day and even if it's not sunny here, 'somewhere,' I say to myself, 'the sun is shining, the clear blue water is gently lapping at the shore edge and a hammock is being gently swayed in the cooling breeze – just not "here". So, in this positive frame of mind I like to think that some women may even reflect upon our recent conversation and either be affirmed by it or appropriately challenged by it. I'm pleased to report that a significant number of women get on the train with a smile on their face and confidence that says, 'I know what I have to do.'

As I walk back to the prison I, too, reflect upon how the 'expedition' to the platform went and sometimes analyse it. I have found myself asking if I could have done more to prevent someone from purchasing their alcohol or going off to find a drug dealer. The usual conclusion I come to is that whatever they did, whether positive or negative, is down to the woman making her choice.

I often review what I'm doing and why, and go back to a set of aims I have devised.

The Aim

There are several reasons why I believe it is important to offer this specific through-the-gate service: personal safety, directions, literacy, public safety and care.

Personal safety: giving support can make vulnerable people feel a little safer from those around them and even from themselves, being distracted from succumbing to the obvious temptations. The women leaving are certainly vulnerable and at risk from each other. Often a dominant woman may try and intimidate another less strong woman into parting with her money or medication – often referred to a 'passing' or making a 'pass'. The pass is often planned for outside the prison and, therefore, being able to link in with someone supportive just outside the gate can reduce the likelihood of being bullied.

Directions: some people don't know where they are going, even after being given very clear directions. I show them the way and either leave them to it or walk along with them.

Literacy: some of the women coming out of prison have very poor literacy skills, so having someone with them who can take them directly without their having to read any road or place names can be reassuring for them. This is the same for people for whom English is a second language. I have escorted a few who have appreciated my talking through slowly what is going to happen at the station and explaining what they need to do once they are on the train, including how many stops they need to count before they should get off.

Public safety: unfortunately there are some people who, having been released from prison, are focused on sharing this specific fact with anyone who is around. They can also occasionally cause a bit of disturbance by swearing, shouting or demonstrating other threatening behaviour – finger gestures in particular. Some women specialise in being rude and like to see how many people they can upset. If a woman has had her money or medication stolen by another released prisoner, this could make her more tempted to steal from a member of the public or shop, in order to recoup what she has lost.

Care: this is not something one might initially think of as an aim, but it's perhaps the most important aspect of the whole process, showing the women that the prison and the chaplaincy team cares about them, regardless of what they have done or who they are. By understanding their frailty, respecting them and their situation, we can demonstrate, with no strings attached, that they are valued for who they are. This is a great way to practically show people God's love for them.

My presence can have a calming effect as well as being informative and supportive. This can also be good news for the prison and their public relations, and possibly even reduce reoffending in the short term.

When I think of all the 'thanks' I get from the women and what appears to be their genuine gratitude, I'm certain that for some people I make a real difference. I often see a transformation from the person I first met inside to the person I see on the train as we wave each other goodbye.

Reflection

Luke 24:30-32

When he was at the table with them, he took bread, gave thanks, broke it and began to give it to them. Then their eyes were opened and they recognised him, and he disappeared from their sight. They asked each other, 'Were not our hearts burning within us while he talked with us on the road and opened the Scriptures to us?'

Eyes opened

I get really excited when I read these few verses, especially 'Were not our hearts burning within us . . .' It's that lightbulb moment, the moment when everything comes together and makes sense. I can just imagine these two travellers looking at each other and knowing they have the same thought; one perhaps beckoning to the other to come aside as they share their revelation.

As I walk with the women the one mile to the train station from the holding cell, I often hear them say that they now see things differently since they have been in prison; the things that they once took for granted, such as being with their children every day or being able to pop out of their home whenever they wanted or to choose when they had a bath or shower and not to worry about time limits and who else might be around. They have had time to reflect on their lives and re-evaluate their priorities. Things now seem clearer; the light has shone brightly and highlighted a change of thought and direction. The journey away from the prison may feel like the beginning of a new chapter for many as they are released from the establishment – a new beginning.

I still remember to this very day how I felt when as an eighteen-year-old I was formally diagnosed with having dyslexia. For the first time I could really believe that I wasn't just 'slow' or 'thick' but everything now made sense. I finally understood why I struggled with certain things; it was a lightbulb moment for me. From that moment on I began to believe in myself a little more and dared to dream of becoming a husband, father and successful at work. However, it was only the beginning of a long journey, one that of course continues to this day.

Questions

1. Can you recall a 'lightbulb' moment and how did you feel?
2. Can you remember a time where you felt you have had a 'new beginning'?
3. What prompted the 'new beginning' and who was there for you?
4. Did you have any fears regarding your 'new beginning'? What were they?

For prayer

Please pray for those people who are starting out on 'new beginnings'. Pray they will overcome their fears and have the support they need. Pray also for 'lightbulb' moments for yourself and others, moments of revelation and clarity, moments that will challenge and motivate you as you go on life's 'journey'.

Chapter 7
What next?

Going back

I debated what the sub-heading should be because I thought 'Going back' sounded too negative and could imply going backwards. I would prefer to think of it meaning going back into the community. But in truth many of the women I walk to the station do actually go straight back to the troubled life they had recently swapped for a prison life. The suggestion that they 'swapped' lives may infer that they had some control, and in a strange way perhaps they did. By continuing along a 'path' of disengagement, drug misuse and crime they know that they will sooner rather than later come back to prison. Some see it as a consequence of their actions whilst a few may view it as part of their journey and therefore expect it or even forecast it. It is like the inevitable stop off at the off-licence at the end of the road leading to the prison: it is there and has to be encountered.

Perhaps this is a good place to remind us that I specialise in working with some of the most troubled and broken women in society, and I count it a privilege. So success as previously mentioned is measured more by the level of engagement than the woman never returning to prison. Sadly, many of the women I journey with have struggled to engage with support agencies, so when we connect and they engage, that, for me, is a very positive step they are making and one to be celebrated.

Naturally I'm pleased when I don't see someone come back but, honestly, I have been walking with women to the station up to five days a week for nearly two years, and prior to that occasionally over a nine-year period, so understandably I can't remember everybody I've said goodbye to; sometimes it's only when they remind me that we walked down the road together last time that my memory is jogged. I am aware that there are many women who after one visit to prison never return. I used to work with them all the time in the chaplaincy department back inside the prison. Sometimes they would write letters to us sharing their 'good news' stories when back with their families, engaging with their faith and in a few cases even having a job. Yet 'good news' for many of the women I engage with is defined by just being alive, especially when they know of so many of their friends who have died young.

I'm not sure whether it is grammatically correct to suggest that there is a level of success graded as 'super-successful' or 'ultra-successful' as success in itself is an ultimate achievement but, in my opinion, that is what the women I meet on the road to the station and who never return to custody are. Some of them have overcome their equivalent of Mount Everest. Their success is amazing.

Unfortunately, a significant number of the women I engage with will finish their journey that day back on familiar ground, taking drugs, beatings and taking life-threatening risks. They hustle, steal, manipulate their way through each day and 'score' (consume illegal or non-prescribed drugs). It is the life they know. Some people race to the station and can't get out of town quick enough or can't get back to their 'patch' quick enough. Others are content with dawdling, taking as long as they can as they are in no hurry to 'work', 'score' and 'crash out'. Back on their territory they begin their daily cycle which is likely to involve getting their dose of prescribed methadone, engaging in activities that will bring in the money they need for the drugs they take and share later. It's a routine they are very familiar with: 'back' for them means back in the old routine.

Seven miles to change direction

Sometimes I want to answer the question 'What next?' with 'Who knows?' This isn't a glib or aggressive statement but one I hope you will now understand. There are many different answers, as complex and varied as those I walk alongside. I'm not blaspheming when I say, 'God only knows.' In some cases I truly believe that only he knows what is going to happen next. As you will have read, I'm often bamboozled, confused and surprised by what happens on the mile to the station; trying to get my head around how that day or week or month may play out for some of the women I encounter is beyond me. But not all women end up back at where they were just prior to prison.

Some women are further along on a journey to restoration and healing than others. When I reflect upon the story of the two on the road to Emmaus I am mindful, as recorded in the previous chapter, that they had to come to a point at which they saw things differently – the lightbulb moment. Over the years, I have been asked on numerous occasions what the secret is to a person stopping their offending behaviour and turning their life around. There is no one answer that is applicable for all offenders. For some it is a change in family circumstances – perhaps the death of a relative or the birth of a grandchild. Sometimes it's finding a place to call home for the first time, getting a job or having a good support network around them and professional intervention such as counselling, or perhaps a 'God moment' – divine revelation and conversion. Sometimes the change begins when they wake up tired and exhausted: 'There has to be more to life than this,' they whisper to themselves. I often put it down to a matter of timing or perhaps to the process of maturing. They have gone so far down the road that they now have to stop, just as the Emmaus two stopped. And it only takes place when the woman is ready to stop. Because we can't always predict when this change of mind will take place or if indeed it ever will; we have to be prepared to offer opportunities and see what happens. I may have walked with the same person a few times before there is a change in the conversation or behaviour, yet I'm always hopeful that it is 'this time' rather than 'next time'. I don't know what God's plans are for the individual standing in front of me, so all I can do is give them my best effort, care as God would have me care for them and pray that the 'miracle' is scheduled for 'today'. Unfortunately resources such as rehabilitation centres and detoxification units are scarce and often very expensive. Therefore, if it is viewed that it is unlikely to aid a particular woman as she is deemed unready for it or she has had this opportunity in the past and it hasn't been 'successful' then, sadly, in some cases very little is available for the woman. For some the journey to recovery can be a long one: it took the two walking with Jesus over seven miles to have the 'new beginnings' moment; it can take people with broken lives and a history of abuse and imprisonment many 'miles' of travel or years of toil before the breakthrough.

I firmly believe that transformation can only take place when the person is ready to engage. The two on the road walking away from Jerusalem engaged with Jesus. Engagement involves a commitment to listen, reflect and share. From that comes a position of trust, hope and belief. When the two reached where they were staying, they finally agreed not only with his views and teaching on the Messiah but they also believed this stranger was Jesus – the Messiah himself. The transformation came from within them: their minds were changed, their doubts addressed and their hope restored.

Seven miles more

The story of the two on the road to Emmaus doesn't end with their lightbulb moment. Immediately, they got up and went back to where they had started out from that day. In essence it is a fourteen-mile round trip story, yet very little is known about their return journey. We can surmise that they were happy and extremely motivated to get back. However, it may be that they were a little embarrassed and rehearsed what they would say to the others when they returned and what they might say to Jesus if they met him again. Perhaps this time as they wandered back they were looking out for him. Having just travelled seven miles and with only a short break, when they returned they may have been exhausted, they may have needed to rest on the walk back. In fact it might have been as equally a difficult journey back as they didn't have the distraction of Jesus engaging them as they walked together and it would have been later in the day. By the time they returned the initial euphoria and adrenalin rush may have subsided and a little fatigue may have set in.

There are stories of women who overcome the most challenging and horrendous of situations, who go through what can be described as 'hell and back again'. My good friend Linda Huskisson has a tremendous story of journeying through abuse of various forms: prostitution, addiction to drugs and alcohol, having her children taken away from her, battling cancer and imprisonment. I thoroughly recommend you read her story in *Cheating Death, Living Life: Linda's Story* by Ralph Turner (River Publishing). As you go through the book it takes you on her amazing journey of transformation. Linda is now a strong Christian and wonderful role model. Her journey took well over 'fourteen miles' and many years. Yet her journey is continuing – she works with vulnerable people, is a platform speaker, a mum and a grandmother. There is a lot to Linda that isn't in her book, but maybe in another one to come? When people leave prison and don't come back, we don't usually get to hear what happens next or, even when we do, we don't get to hear the detail of their journey: the ups and downs, the failings and the overcoming, the support, pain and joy they have experienced.

Chez

A few months ago I met Chez who was visiting the church I attend. As I looked at her there was something familiar about her, so when I found out she had been a resident in the prison I work in I wasn't too surprised. She is now a very strong Christian and lives a transformed life. However, several years ago she had issues with addictions which led her into prison. Whilst she went to the church services inside, it wasn't to worship but to trade drugs and meet friends. This is very common and something we are all well aware of but grateful that, for whatever the reason, people still attend the services. We always hope that a 'seed' of some form will be sown. Unfortunately, Chez didn't have a miraculous conversion in prison but at least we didn't put her off church.

However, some years after leaving prison she made a commitment to God and is now a wonderful example of God's grace and mercy. As I talked to her I was really blessed and encouraged as she radiated Jesus' love and it was contagious. Although we talked for a long time I didn't get to hear all of her story. There was a huge 'bit' we didn't get around to. I don't know how many times she 'fell' and got 'up' again, what pain she went through and battles she overcame. All I know is that she is now going strong with God, hallelujah! Her story is one that can be told by many women, we just don't get to hear of them all.

The Samaritan woman

I never tire of reading the story of when Jesus talked to a woman in Samaria as found in John 4:1-42. This is a remarkable story for many reasons, especially as it was frowned upon for a man to talk to a woman and especially a Samaritan – Jews and Samaritans did not get on too well at that time. As the conversation develops it is clear the woman has some understanding of the 'Messiah' and that he is going to appear one day. Jesus discloses to her that he is the Messiah and that her life can be different. He even knows without her telling him that she has had five husbands and the person she is currently living with is not her husband. At the end of the story she knows him to be the Messiah and brings others from the village to meet him.

There are many points and various sermons than can be preached from this passage. I'm constantly drawn to the fact that the woman is likely to have known much pain in her life, after all she has had five husbands and my wife says one is enough! We can't presume they have all died so it is likely that some of them ended in divorce. At that time divorce was the prerogative of the male and the wife often had little choice. With five failed marriages and the possible shame of 'living' with someone who wasn't her husband, it is possible to think she had experienced a hard life at times. What a life journey she had been on prior to meeting Jesus and having her own 'lightbulb' moment. When Jesus leaves the village a few days later, we don't know what happens to the woman or the others who are transformed by their encounter with him.

Sometimes we only see a 'snapshot' of a person's life. It is as if we rub shoulders for a short while before going our separate ways. I see women as they come out of what might be described as the worst time of their life. I may know very little of what went on before or after I have engaged with them. It may be that we meet halfway along their life story. I have journeyed with women who have sadly died not long after leaving prison. Recently I walked with a woman who was twenty years old, so hopefully she has many years ahead that won't involve prison but we just don't know.

My 'what next?'

This book has three stories interwoven. The focus is on the women who leave prison and all that this entails. As we have looked at the women's journeys we have reflected upon the journey of the two on the road to Emmaus and there is still more to come. So perhaps it is good for me to reflect a little on the third story – my own.

I have had various 'lightbulb' moments, and invariably these lead to a different way of thinking or even a change of lifestyle or place of employment. Looking at the road to Emmaus passage I am probably at the point of having returned to the group and am sharing my experiences with those around me. I thoroughly enjoy encouraging others, just as the two encouraged those they found back in Jerusalem. As they told their story of meeting Jesus so I enjoy telling mine. I made a firm commitment to 'follow' Jesus after seeing a Christian film when I was sixteen years old and just before I joined the Army. I knelt down beside my bed that night and had a long chat. 'We've chatted' over the years and there have been times when I have felt very close to God and times when I've felt a million miles away. The truth is that God is only one prayer away at any time; it's just that I haven't always spared the time.

Right now I have been drawn closer to God as I have written this book and it has been great to reflect on what God has done in my life and how he is using me at this present time. I want to encourage more people as I continue to share the story of the women as they are released from prison and see amazing things happen. I want to hear about lives miraculously turned around – about 'lightbulb' moments and new beginnings. I want to keep

smiling into the lives of those struggling and keep fist bumping people who need a new experience. I once fist bumped a former Director General of the Ghana Prisons Service! I explained to him how I fist bump the women I work with and asked his permission to fist bump him; he consented. It was as meaningful to do that with him as it is with every woman I engage with. It is my way of saying 'let's get out of our comfort zones and connect'. That particular fist bump with the Director General was challenging for me as I have always struggled with people in positions of authority. I often don't know what to say and stutter or come out with things that aren't really relevant. I'm much more comfortable speaking to the women in prison than those in official positions, especially when unprepared. So fist bumping the Director General was me pushing myself out of my comfort zone. I'm not sure what being out of my comfort zone will look like in the future – perhaps I'll fist bump royalty, presidents and prime ministers, and even very intelligent people with lots of initials after their names. I'm not comfortable dressed up in posh suits or having to make small talk with those in 'high office', so maybe God will send me to meet the Queen one day and test me on my coping skills. I'm not sure how a fist bump with the Queen will go down though – could be interesting? All I can say is, 'I'm here, God, use me as you wish and send me wherever you want me to go.' I was recently asked why I do this particular job by a Governor-grade Prison Service manager. My response was quick and simple: 'Because I love people.' I love to love people and whatever I do I hope that remains – it was how I was made.

Love

That's it, I've sold out! I've used the 'L' word again! So much of this book has been about the harshness of leaving prison. I have talked in terms of painful and sometimes aggressive behaviours and now I spoil it all by going soft. But the truth is love isn't always 'pink' with love hearts and gushing poetry. 'Love' goes into dark places. The author Bob Goff writes about this kind of love in his books *Love Does* and *Everybody Always* (both published by Nelson Books). Love can be whimsical and resilient at the same time. I'm not going to quote from the books as I'd have to fill in forms to get permission, and forms and I don't always get on, but the books are well worth a read and as the titles say: *love does, everybody, always.*

Wouldn't it be great if some of the women instead of using other four-letter words would use 'love'? 'What the love are you doing here?' How challenging would it be if someone said, 'Nobody gives a love about me'? Perhaps as we journey with each other, some people can see God's practical love shining through.

The miracle question

I often find myself asking a woman what a miracle would look like in her life – if she woke up tomorrow and a miracle had occurred how she would know. Some women talk about reconnecting with their families and others talk about being drug free. One woman said recently that she would wake up not thinking about drugs.

I have asked myself this question in relation to work: what miracle would I like to see happen? The answer is simple: that all the women who leave 'my' prison would have somewhere safe to stay, would want to engage with all the services on offer, would not come back to prison, would have a great support network around them, would reconnect healthily with family and friends, would feel positive about their future, would be busy every day, would leave prison not feeling hungry (perhaps because if they didn't have breakfast in the prison there would be a local café that would offer a free meal), they would all have at least one change of clothing (perhaps they would be able to choose from the top range of our local charity shops in town – we don't have a clothing store), be financially stable and full of confidence. I said the answer is simple; seeing it happen would be amazing, perhaps unbelievable! You might say, 'Simeon, get real – that is never going to happen.' And that is why it is my miracle! Of course, I could add that everyone also comes to faith and that those who don't have anywhere safe to stay could temporarily lodge at a hostel in the same town as the prison – something the local authority, local probation service and possibly the local community would all be against as all would understandably argue that they simply don't have the resources. However, that is also part of the miracle, that God provides all the resources as well as the significant mind-changes that are required. Now that would take us all out of our comfort zone!

Comfort zones

Going back into the community and doing what some of us may define as ordinary is scary for some of the women coming out of prison. It may have been a long time since a woman has been able to really trust someone. She may have forgotten what it is like to be cared for as a person in her own right and not as an object to be abused. She may not be used to choosing when she does things or not having to ask for permission. She may not know what it is like to have a full night's rest as when she is outside she has to be ready to fend off someone at a moment's notice or she may not know what it is like to have a regular sleep pattern.

Just re-engaging with society can place a woman outside her comfort zone. So expecting her to settle in straight away is to not understand the journey she may have been on. It can take days if not weeks to acclimatise to a different regime and to get the sound of keys rattling out of her head. And this is the case for most people regardless of if they have complex needs. Expecting people to immediately comply with a change of rules – tailored to living back in society – can be a little unrealistic. Some people don't understand the rules or in some cases have a recent history of breaking them, so expecting them to miraculously change their ways overnight might be asking the impossible. However, there are people returning from prison who work hard at re-adjusting to society and they are to be commended.

Of course, encouraging people who have no background or history of prison engagement to somehow connect with prisoners or those recently released is also an 'out of the comfort zone' experience. We are all drawn to things we are familiar with and many of us struggle with things we are unaccustomed to. Knowing what to say, how to present, what is allowed and what is not can be daunting. I know that when I show people around the prison who have never been to one before, they can be very uneasy about what they can and cannot do, double checking with me if it is permitted to talk to the 'residents' or go onto a 'wing' when invited? Yet for those of us familiar with prisons, we are a little more relaxed about such things. Journeying in unfamiliar environments can be challenging for everyone.

Reflection

Luke 24:33-35

They got up and returned at once to Jerusalem. There they found the Eleven and those with them, assembled together and saying, 'It is true! The Lord has risen and has appeared to Simon.' Then the two told what had happened on the way, and how Jesus was recognised by them when he broke the bread.

Returning

I wonder what the two thought they would find when they returned to the group. Perhaps they were thinking someone might say 'I told you so' when they shared that Jesus was alive and well. Perhaps there may have been one or two in the group who thought that their leaving everyone in Jerusalem and 'walking away' was wrong or inappropriate. Maybe they were scared about what the others may have thought about them. Or perhaps they didn't care and just wanted to be with everyone again, excited about sharing their 'lightbulb' experience. We don't know if they gave any thought to what was to come next, but we do know they returned at once having had their 'lightbulb' moment.

I remember what it was like returning from the Army after just three months. For the first two or so weeks I marched around everywhere and waited to be told what time I needed to do things. I was ready to receive orders and comply, but not to think for myself.

For many women returning is scary, especially those who have a history of not lasting long outside and complying with a regime they can't cope with. I'm sure the fear of 'what next' or concerns about how it is all going to turn out for them is very present in their thoughts as they continue on life's journey.

Questions

1. Have you ever returned somewhere and wondered about what you would find?
2. How do you cope with not knowing what is happening next?
3. Can you think of an experience that took you out of your comfort zone?
4. How did you feel at the time and how did you cope with it?

For prayer

Please pray for those people returning from prison who are worried about how they will cope and what others may think of them. Pray that they will continue on their journey of rehabilitation no matter what obstacles they come across and that they keep going, however long it may take. Pray for those people you know who are currently journeying outside of their comfort zone, pray that God will guide them and protect them.

Chapter 8
Getting Alongside

Peace

When we look at the story of the two on the road to and from Emmaus, focusing on verses 36 to 39 we note that Jesus got alongside the two of them twice. Whilst the first time they didn't recognise him, the second time when he appeared in front of them and the others gathered together he made sure they all knew it was him and his opening words were, '*Peace be with you.*'

Peace is something that many of us crave and if we are lucky some of us find it on occasions. Yet for the women I work with peace is often elusive and just out of reach. Some never know what it is like to have peace of mind or rest in their bodies or to exist in a peaceful environment. As Jesus stood there amongst them he knew some would be afraid or confused so his first words were of reassurance. We all need reassurance at times and perhaps those people for whom hope has been lost need comfort and assurance most. Jesus then went on to demonstrate that it was really him standing in front of them. He invited them to touch him, to reach out and connect in the most undeniable way, by physically touching his wounds. I am reminded of how the woman with bleeding reached out and touched the hem of Jesus' cloak and was healed from twelve years of pain, rejection and disappointment – see Luke 8:43-44. I have often preached this in the prison, encouraging the women to reach out in prayer to Jesus and asking him to heal and restore them. In verse 48 Jesus says, 'Daughter, your faith has healed you. Go in peace.' Jesus invites and affirms all those who reach out to him and is ready to bring peace into confusing situations.

Ileana

It was a busy morning in the prison's discharge area, there had been many people going off to court and therefore many vans in and out of the prison and it certainly wasn't peaceful. Now there were seven women waiting to be released, three of whom were very excited and quite chaotic in their behaviour: getting up and sitting down, asking questions and not listening to the answers, packing and unpacking their bags. The other four looked on, hoping not to be caught up in the frenzied activity surrounding them.

I was called to the counter and introduced to Ileana, who it was clear was struggling with everything going on around her. She was a foreign national with limited English. It was explained to her by the prison officers that I would help her get to the train station. I gestured to her, pointed at the two of us with my index finger and then attempted my best two-fingers walking motion and ended the mime with the wheels of an old-fashioned train going around and around. She nodded and I smiled and said, 'OK?' She replied, 'OK.' This appeared to calm her agitation for a short while.

When the main gate rolled back I was standing waiting for Ileana, unfortunately her anxiety had come back as she said 'no phone' several times and then 'children'. She pointed to the other women, some of whom had their phones and then pointed back to the prison. In my calmest and most reassuring voice I said, 'OK, don't worry, come with me,' and tried to encourage her towards the coffee shop, from where I knew I could sort things out. She understandably became more flustered, probably imaging that I was taking her down to the station with no phone and therefore with no way of contacting her children. I placed my two hands in front of me – palms down and gently motioned to slow down and relax a little. I then gestured that I would make a telephone call and pointed to the coffee shop. As soon as we got into the coffee shop, which took no more than thirty seconds to reach, she was reminding me she had no phone. Some of her mannerisms could have appeared forceful or even a little aggressive but I took this as a sign of stress as well as appreciating different countries have different styles of communication, some being blunt and more assertive than others. Her tone was certainly sharp as she repeatedly mentioned her phone.

Once inside the building I showed her the coffee shop's phone and said that I would ring over to the prison – all said with the appropriated gestures. However, two of the three chaotic women had also come with us in to the coffee shop and needed a little assistance and direction. This slowed my phoning the prison a little and again Ileana was certainly on my case. Eventually, the other two left to walk to the station with an experienced volunteer, leaving me to concentrate on Ileana and the phone. She was extremely relieved when I put the phone down and with a smile and a thumbs-up gesture said the phone was still in the prison and we could collect it. Together we walked the short distance back to the gatehouse and waited for someone to bring it over to us.

Ileana was pleased but this only lasted a minute: the battery was dead. As we walked into the coffee shop I did my best 'calm down it's going to be OK' gesture. We keep phone chargers under the counter for situations such as this. Yet again she didn't think I understood her dilemma until the plug and cable were produced. Finally she got through on the phone to her family and a more relaxed presence came over her.

Eventually, having consumed a drink of hot chocolate whilst waiting for the phone to charge a little and having used the toilet, we got to the station. The chaotic two had missed one train and were there with the volunteer as we arrived. The volunteer had done a great job of calming one of them down; the other one was walking up and down the station but keeping herself to herself. I assisted Ileana in getting her warrant converted into a ticket and showed her on a train map where she was going and how many stops this was. She had to change when she got to the last station in London and get a train on the Underground, so I wrote down on a piece of paper the Underground line and station she needed and told her – accompanied with the necessary gestures – to show someone in uniform the note so she could get further help. Ileana finally got on the train a lot more relaxed and at peace than when I met her in prison an hour and a half before.

Over the years there have been several women I have needed to reassure and confusing situations where I have worked hard to bring peace; Ileana's experience was just one of many. I believe I'm not only a bag carrier and a walking signpost but also a peace bearer, bringing calm to traumatic situations.

And what can I do?

I have heard over the years people say, 'I would like to get involved but I don't think I'm cut out for this kind of work.' I have often said that I know I'm not cut out to be a prison officer and have total respect for the work they do but it's not for me. I'm far better suited to work as a chaplain than anything else in a prison. My character and skillset are a good match for this line of work. When responding to someone wanting to get involved, I encourage them to reflect upon what their motivation is and what skills or qualities they have to offer.

Volunteer

On several occasions in the book I have referred to the volunteers who have assisted me as I journey with the women, some come from local churches or through word of mouth or from organisations such as Mothers' Union. Not everyone who volunteers is of faith. Prisons are no strangers to welcoming volunteers. Over the centuries there have been people who have got involved in prisons and championed the reformation of the criminal justice sector. Historically, Christians have played a significant part. Jesus' story of the sheep and the goats in Matthew 25:31-46 highlights his concern for those in prison and has served as a great encouragement to so many.

As the scope of what is undertaken has developed over the years in prisons, so has the use of volunteers. They can be found in various departments including chaplaincy and education, assisting in supporting those running classes as well as offering a little extra one-to-one support when required. Most volunteers are expected to undergo training and have the necessary vetting completed before they roll up their sleeves and get involved. This is also the case with the volunteers who support me.

Volunteers come with a range of life experiences, skills and motivation. Some now have time on their hands and want to use their knowledge or experience in a way that will benefit people who perhaps could appear 'less' fortunate than them. Yet on the other hand there are people who volunteer precisely because they themselves were once in a spot of bother and had someone come alongside them and support them to get through their specific challenges. Having had that experience, they now find themselves in a position where they can offer the type of help they once received.

Nowadays volunteers work not only inside prisons but also when the prisoners are released. They assist in various types of through-the-gate projects including taking people recently released to their appointments and becoming mentors and befrienders once the person is back in their community.

However, I don't recommend people volunteer in a prison-related ministry if they can't cope with inconsistency and sudden change as prison life and prisoners themselves can be a little chaotic and unpredictable at times. Having read this book you will appreciate the women I specialise in supporting can be very challenging and I advise against people assisting me if they can't be mentally flexible at a moment's notice and robust as they see and hear things that can be somewhat shocking. Yet when these things happen we of course debrief and take time to reflect and unwind; it is really important to support each other. Only the other day we walked a woman to the station who shared how her mother introduced her to drugs and how she had known a lot of pain and trauma. This challenged the volunteer I was with.

There are various ways to get started as a volunteer in prison. If you don't already have any connection with your local prison but feel you want to offer yourself as a volunteer then ring the prison's switchboard and ask if there is a volunteer coordinator or anyone there who oversees volunteers. Many chaplaincy teams oversee Official Prison Visitors and some will oversee generic volunteers as well, so if there is no specific coordinator then ask to be put through to the chaplaincy team. A simple search on the internet will enable you to locate your nearest prison and its switchboard telephone number. If, however, you already know someone who is connected to the prison, speak to them about your interest. This process, though, can challenge your resolve to get involved as it may take months before you are in there as a regular volunteer. And please don't tell the chaplain that you want to come into the prison and preach the gospel and lead people to Jesus. What chaplains really want to hear is someone saying, 'Here I am, I'm available and have these skills – can you use them?' Take it from me that the gospel is already preached and people do make commitments of faith when in prison.

If you want to volunteer in the community by supporting people at a local level who have come out of prison then a simple search online should help you identify local organisations involved in this service. Useful search words are: support for prisoners / ex-prisoners / community support / and your town's name, or contact your local prison or probation service who may be able to let you know what organisations operate locally. One such group that operates in London (UK) is Caring for Ex-Offenders (www. caringforexoffenders.org), a Christian organisation that supports ex-offenders. Their criteria for involvement with ex-offenders are that they are:

- resettling to Greater London (UK),
- willing to be supported by Christians, and
- have expressed a desire to change.

There are also many non-Christian organisations that support people coming out of prison.

Pray

All Christians are called to pray for those in need. And this is the best place to start if you are asking God if you could or should get involved in prison ministry. Everyone can pray for those in prison, both in the UK and globally. It's not just in the UK, but in many countries around the world there are issues with people who are coming out of prison. Intolerance, discrimination, underfunding and lack of resources are commonplace, regardless of the wealth or development of the country. There are too few resources for people coming out of prison who are motivated to change, and even fewer for those who live a chaotic lifestyle. I have no idea how many services there are globally that specialise in supporting people on an ad hoc basis on the day of their release, and in particular those who have no one to meet them, but I would imagine it's very few. This is an area that needs to be addressed both locally and globally.

General issues to pray about include:

Prisoners / residents: pray for those people new to prison, those who are separated from families and loved ones, support for those with illnesses and disabilities, that the prisoner / resident will get the support they require inside to address their offending behaviour, that they may maintain contact with key people outside, that they will be motivated to make the best of their time inside, that support will be available when they are released and that they take advantage of it. Please pray also for all those being released, especially for their first day outside.

Prisoner's families: that they will remain in contact with the prisoner / resident and will themselves be supported as they cope with the situation in the community – many are also victims of the prisoner / resident.

Victims: that they and those around them will be given all the support they require. Pray that they will recover from the ordeal they have encountered and learn to live without the constant memory of what they have experienced.

Professionals: pray for those supporting serving prisoners / residents / former prisoners; that they will be given all the resources they need to offer the appropriate level of support to those inside and outside of prison.

Police and courts: that they carry out their duties as best they can, with the support and resources required.

Hopefully you are now aware of many of the issues that face women upon their release. Some issues are also common for men, including: accommodation, finances, work or purposeful daily activities, professional support, local support (including people who can offer time to listen), that families are reconnected when it is appropriate. Pray against addictions and pray for good health and medical support. Pray that those people who have a faith will get the support they require and grow in their faith. May I suggest that if you can't pray every day, a good day to pray for prisoners being released is on a Friday. Fridays are often the busiest day as those who have a release day of Saturday or Sunday are also released on Fridays (no releases usually take place at the weekend). It can be very difficult for people released on a Friday as many support services are not open at the weekend, so they have to 'survive' a few days before they can access help. I've heard women say they would be happy to have been held inside over the weekend rather than being released on a Friday.

The are several organisations that can help you to pray knowledgably.

Prisons Week: (www.prisonsweek.org) is an annual week and organisation that focuses on issues relating to those in prison, their victims, families and those working in the criminal justice sector. They provide a prayer leaflet and resources to accompany the week that in the UK is usually held in October.

Prison Fellowship (England and Wales): (www.prisonfellowship. org.uk) is a Christian ministry that oversees prayer and practical support for local prisons. They will be able to advise as to where the nearest prayer group is or send out regular prayer pointers.

Prison Fellowship International: (www.pfi.org) is a good place to start if you want to pray or get involved with prison ministry around the world.

Give financially

There are dozens of organisations nationally and locally that work with people who are in prison, on their way out or have been in prison and are now established in the community but need financial support. Many good projects come to an end or are never developed fully due to the withdrawal or lack of funding. If you have money you wish to donate then an internet search may help you with where and how you would like to donate it.

Employment

There is an ever-growing number of national companies prepared to employ people with a criminal conviction, however the number is still extremely small and more are needed. Employees who have a criminal record can be some of the most motivated members of staff because they don't take their employment for granted and very much appreciate their employers giving them the opportunity to engage back into society.

If you are an employer or think the company or organisation you work for would be interested in employing people with a criminal record then there are several organisations that can offer advice and support. One of these is Clean Sheet (www.cleansheet. org.uk). They support men and women into sustainable employment after they leave prison and will give companies all the support they require if they choose to employ people with convictions.

Accommodation

Finding and maintaining accommodation for people who have come out of prison is as you will now appreciate an extremely challenging process and almost impossible at times. Many private landlords do not want to accept people receiving benefits of any form. If you are a private landlord or know someone who is, or even have a substantial amount of money to invest in property and feel God could be calling you to get involved in this area, then there are various Christian organisations that assist landlords in renting out their properties to people who have been in prison. One of these organisations is Hope into Action (www. hopeintoaction.org.uk).

Lobbying and research

You may be someone who when they understand a cause are keen to get involved and raise relevant issues with people and organisations in power and positions of authority. A search online may help you identify those organisations involved in lobbying. You may also consider contacting your local Member of Parliament and expressing your thoughts on the subject of supporting people who come out of prison.

Should you want to know more about what Christian organisations are working in the criminal justice sector or hear more stories relating to those who have experienced prison and have changed their lives around, may I suggest you visit your local Christian bookshop, if you have one, for specialist input. They often act as a local hub and are likely to know what ministries are operating locally which may also help you to get involved if this is a direction you are wishing to take. I'm blessed to be involved in a local independent shop – Canaan Christian Ministries (www.canaanchristianministries.co.uk). Sadly, there are a decreasing number of Christian bookshops in the UK so please be encouraged to go to your local shop and ask them for recommended reading material and local information.

What can my church do?

Whilst most Christians would agree that supporting people in the margins of society is something they believe the church is called to do, many wouldn't know where to start, especially in supporting people who have just come out of prison. Working with people who have had criminal convictions or have spent time in prison can be rewarding and challenging. Churches need to be honest with themselves as to what they can offer and also be prepared for the difficulties that may arise.

Before your church gets involved with people known to the criminal justice system it might be wise to contact their denominations headquarters or diocese or regional headquarters as they may have experts working with such people already and can offer practical advice. There may also be members of your congregation who may have local expertise such as police officers, magistrates, social workers, probation and prison officers.

When thinking about what your church can offer to people coming out of prison there are several things to consider.

Making worship accessible: it can be a scary thing to walk into a church where you don't know anyone, especially if you have just come out of prison. Providing a friendly welcome, someone to meet them for a coffee before the service and then sit with them when they attend worship for the first time is a big help. This is exactly how I started my involvement with people known to the prison system. I was asked by my church to mentor someone coming out of prison and befriend them; to meet them before the service and sit with them during it as support – this then grew into a friendship. Some people coming out of prison may have poor levels of literacy, so may need help with service sheets and hymn books or reading from the screen in front. People with an alcohol addiction may need the option of non-alcoholic communion wine if it's not routinely used.

Befriending / pastoral care: the care structures in your church may be able to provide a listening ear, friendship and help with issues like filling in forms. As mentioned previously, I certainly need help with form filling. However, people taking on these roles, 'working' alongside people with complex needs, will need to be well supported and trained to understand the need for boundaries.

Mentoring: some churches will train people as mentors, offering a range of help and encouragement, with regular meetings and a long-term commitment. Training for this is available from secular and Christian organisations.

Purposeful activity: people who have recently come out of prison need to use their time productively. It is hard to get a job with a criminal record and keeping busy helps keep people out of trouble. Getting involved with anything the church is running can help people fill their time as well as learn new skills and gain confidence. However, care needs to be taken in finding activities that are suitable in view of the person's previous convictions.

Social life: it is important that people coming out of prison stay away from old associates who are not a good influence and make new friends who will hopefully model a healthier way of living. Some people may have been moved to a new area where they don't know anyone and need to make new friends. Churches can often help provide a positive social environment for new beginnings.

Spiritual support: some people will have come to faith in prison or have renewed past commitments. Many will have been involved in faith activities through prison chaplaincy and will have attended regular services and Bible studies. Growing in faith can be a significant motivator to changing your behaviour and that is certainly the case for many who have been in prison. Opportunities for small group study, access to Bible study notes or literature and one-to-one input may be appropriate and helpful.

Prison visiting: if someone you have been working with ends up back in prison, it can be a real encouragement if people visit or write to them. This can help them feel able to return to church when they are released and can encourage them to address their offending behaviour whilst in prison.

Raise the profile of prison ministry: your church may consider developing a prison ministry team that can engage with the nearest prison or, if it is too far away, then at least commit to praying for it regularly. Your church may also consider participating in the annual Prisons Week by hosting speakers, perhaps from the nearest Prison Fellowship group and circulating the annual handout.

What does the church need to be aware of?

Being realistic: your church needs to be honest and realistic about what it can provide. It is better to start small, rather than offer all sorts of support it cannot maintain. People who have come out of prison need churches to be reliable and consistent, which will include being able to offer long-term support. Churches need time to learn and develop the skills and resources to work effectively with this specific group.

The church will also need to be realistic about the people joining them from prison. They may have a sincere Christian faith, but changing behaviour is often difficult with many ups and downs and doesn't always happen overnight. Some people released do reoffend and may end up back in prison. A few people will struggle with long-term mental health issues, family problems or drug and alcohol addiction. Moving to a more positive lifestyle may take a long time for some individuals. Sometimes little steps are what is needed and not necessarily a rapid or dramatic change, although for some this is exactly what happens. A Christian faith does not guarantee they will address all their problems and never reoffend.

Aware of other church members: it is important that church leaders are aware of others in their congregation who may have been victims of crime or have victims of crime in their families. Others may struggle with having less than perfectly behaved newcomers as part of their church community. Some members of the congregation may be vulnerable to giving inappropriate help – such as giving money or inviting strangers to share their home – and could perhaps easily become victims of fraud or theft. They may need advice and support to ensure they are kept safe.

Know your newcomer: some people recently out of prison are unlikely to ever offend again and need just a little help in getting back on their feet. Sadly, a few people will continue to commit offences. It is always helpful to access additional information when available. This might be through probation or CRC officers, a community drug or mental health team, although the person themselves may need to give permission for you to be given this personal information.

Be aware of the risks: most newcomers are great! But a few will have some challenging behaviour which the church needs to be aware of. All churches should have clear guidelines as to how to safeguard vulnerable people within the church community and how to manage those people with convictions that can put people at risk.

Keep clear boundaries: people may need to be reminded of what personal information to give out. This can include what is on notice boards and in newssheets – such as names and addresses and who is in hospital. People may also need to be reminded not to give money over to people they don't really know.

Balance: there should always be a period of 'weighing up' any newcomer from anywhere. Just because a person dresses smartly or talks with an educated accent and has never been in trouble with the criminal justice system doesn't mean they may not have their own personal struggles which could impact and challenge the church. And just because another newcomer may have had a 'run in' with the criminal justice system doesn't mean they are going to challenge the church either. They may become fantastic members of the family and a superb asset. Their history and experience may be an absolute blessing to the church.

The Welcome Directory (www.welcomedirectory.org.uk) is an organisation that supports faith groups committed to welcoming people who have come out of prison. They will be able to offer a lot of support and advice on this subject.

Reflection

Luke 24:36-49

While they were still talking about this, Jesus himself stood among them and said to them, 'Peace be with you.'

They were startled and frightened, thinking they saw a ghost. He said to them, 'Why are you troubled, and why do doubts rise in your minds? Look at my hands and my feet. It is I myself! Touch me and see; a ghost does not have flesh and bones, as you see I have.'

When he had said this, he showed them his hands and feet. And while they still did not believe it because of joy and amazement, he asked them, 'Do you have anything here to eat?' They gave him a piece of broiled fish, and he took it and ate it in their presence.

He said to them, 'This is what I told you while I was still with you: everything must be fulfilled that is written about me in the Law of Moses, the Prophets and the Psalms.'

Then he opened their minds so they could understand the Scriptures. He told them, 'This is what is written: the Messiah will suffer and rise from the dead on the third day, and repentance for the forgiveness of sins will be preached in his name to all nations, beginning at Jerusalem. You are witnesses of these things. I am going to send you what my Father has promised; but stay in the city until you have been clothed with power from on high.'

The body of Christ

In the passage above we read that on the day of Jesus' resurrection his followers *'were startled and frightened'* when they saw him standing before them. However, shortly afterwards he is saying, *'This is what is written: the Messiah will suffer and rise from the dead on the third day, and repentance for the forgiveness of sins will be preached in his name to all nations, beginning at Jerusalem. You are witnesses of these things. I am going to send you what my Father has promised; but stay in the city until you have been clothed with power from on high.'* We know from Pentecost onwards the disciples and followers of Jesus ministered in great power and healings and miracles were performed.

Today we are called to be Christ's body here on Earth and to move in his power.

1 Corinthians 12:27-28

Now you are the body of Christ, and each one of you is a part of it. And God has placed in the church first of all apostles, second prophets, third teachers, then miracles, then gifts of healing, of helping, of guidance, and of different kinds of tongues.

I believe we should move in the same power as Jesus did and I am yet again reminded of the story of Jesus with the woman who suffered from twelve years of bleeding. When she reached out and touched the hem of his cloak the power went out of him (see Luke 9:46). I think the church should be accessible for people in need of restoration to reach out and receive a life-changing encounter. In every town I would like to think there are Christians who can minister in power to those who have recently come out of prison. Yet in order to do this we need to know of the need and what support we can give, what difference we can make? One of the reasons for writing this book has been to raise the specific issues of people coming out of prison, in particular women, some of whom may have had chaotic lifestyles and as a result need extra care and support.

Questions

1. Do you believe in the power of prayer and have you witnessed prayers being answered? If so, what happened?
2. Can you think of a time when you received prayer for something that had taken control of your life and you have struggled to break free from it?
3. How did you feel knowing people were praying for you?
4. Have you ever prayed for people in prison or for those involved in the criminal justice system? If not, will you now?

For prayer

Please pray for churches to be better equipped to minster to those people returning from prison and to be accessible. Pray for prisoners' families and for victims of crime. Pray also for all those professionals and agencies involved in supporting people in the criminal justice system.

Chapter 9
Walking On

Bridget

I met Bridget today; she was in the holding cell with six others. I recognised five of them, knowing I had walked with three of them in the recent past. Bridget sat there quietly with her back to the window. It was an early summer's morning and whilst the sun was shining through the window I knew there was a breeze accompanying it. As I usually do, I went around the group introducing myself to those I didn't recognise, confirming with the others that they knew what I did.

When I got to Bridget her first words were, 'Simeon, I thought you'd left?' I explained my journey to her and how I was back again and what I do now. 'Is that what you were doing when I saw you at the station a while ago?' she asked. I remembered Bridget but didn't remember the recent engagement. I remembered her from a few years ago when she was regularly attending our church services in the chapel. As I sat alongside her I was aware she wasn't as relaxed as I had seen her in the past. She went on to tell me that she wasn't ready to be released this time; she had only been in prison for two weeks as she was on a licence recall. Our conversation got interrupted and she slumped back into her chair.

I wanted to spend more time with Bridget but there was one woman who wanted to show me photographs of her mother and daughter and I felt privileged to be given a viewing. And then there was another woman who was highly strung and taking up not only a lot of space in the room but dominating the conversation. Eventually the woman who was placing herself at the centre of everything was called to the counter and I resumed my chat with Bridget. She asked what the weather was like outside, noting the sun in the sky, but there was little else to spot from the holding cell window other than concrete and very little air coming through the air-vent. I said it was a little chilly for the time of year and this worried her slightly as she had no coat. I suggested that if she wasn't in a hurry to get to the station she could pop into the coffee shop with me and look through a small rack of spare donated coats to see if anything took her fancy. She agreed to this as she was in no hurry to go anywhere as she was not on any form of licence and didn't need to report to a probation office. Neither did she have an address to go to, so hanging around with me was fine by her. I told her about the Salvation Army and the 'homeless' bag they give out and she seemed very keen to go in there as well.

Finally, all seven were released. The domineering woman continued to vie for attention. She was unsure as to whether she would be able to walk to the station or get a minicab there. In the end I suggested the volunteer with me that day took care of her while I concentrated on Bridget. The other woman eventually got a minicab and I got some quality time with Bridget. Together we strolled over to the coffee shop, ordered a coffee and looked through some coats. There was a designer-labelled garment which not only was a good fit but matched the colour of her outfit. She was delighted with it; a great big smile came over her face again as she thanked me for this and the drink. Three of the other releases were inside the shop as well, and Bridget knew that hanging around with them would only lead her to get up to 'things', the very 'things' she was battling. So we decided to walk to the station separately, keeping well away from the off-licence.

We dropped into the Salvation Army and picked up the bag and some food. Bridget was delighted and her heaviness began to lighten. She was now talking in terms of God looking after her today and this spirit continued as we journeyed together. When we came to the Anglican church I invited her to write her name on the art installation outside. The church decided to keep it in place over the summer period. She signed it and really appreciated that there was another church that was ready to engage with her. She loved the thought that her name was noted and she'd be prayed for. At the station her mood was altogether more positive than when we first met and she asked me to pray for her there and then, which I did. Bridget then talked about her options, where she could go for specific support; she knew where she could get food and a shower and said she was known to an outreach project. She once again thanked me and reflected on all the support she had received as she was released from prison – a free coffee, the 'homeless' person's bag, encouraged to know people were going to pray for her and all my help. Just before the train pulled in I told her that I was writing this book and asked if I could write about her, albeit changing her name. She agreed and said she thought it would be a good read and a message that really needed sharing with others, and that she would look out for it and buy a copy. She asked when it would be published. I said I didn't know and she replied that she'd keep looking anyway. We waved goodbye and then it hit me! She had responded to my support and encouragement by supporting and encouraging me. I walked away feeling fantastic.

When we first spoke that day Bridget was feeling very unready for the outside world and understandably a little self-absorbed. When we parted she was thinking about me, my project and wishing me well. In just over one hour and one mile her demeanour and focus had altered. I then thought about the two followers of Jesus as they journeyed alongside him and how their understanding and focus had also altered, to the point where they turned themselves around. It was their choice to go straight back. As a result, by the end of their day they were back with the other believers. My hope and prayer is that at the end of that particular day Bridget had been able to turn herself around and connect with people who could support her, but I don't know.

As I've noted before, the reality is that I just don't know what happens to the women I have journeyed with. Sometimes I wish I did and sometimes I think I'm glad not to know. Are Bridget or Emmy, Marcia, Di, Leanne and Kirsty, Dee, Keesh, Tina and Al, Loz or Ileana safe tonight? I don't know but God does and I have to leave all those I have walked alongside to him. But I know that for some people I have made a difference and I thank God for that.

Who knows

As you know, there have been hundreds of people who have left the prison I work in over the years and never come back. Only a handful like Chez do we ever hear about. Those we've lost touch with are out there getting on with their lives and I wouldn't be surprised if only a few of their closest people know that they had spent time in prison.

There have been several women that I have met who appear to be journeying in what might be seen as the 'wrong' direction and yet, as a result of our meeting, they present as leaving a little more encouraged and hopeful. What I have learnt from my experience of walking with the women is to never judge or predict. I have been surprised so many times in the past that these days I'm a lot slower to forecast how things are going to play out. If you, too, are journeying with someone who is struggling or heading in a direction and are filled with fear, please keep journeying with them, if only in prayer – never give up on them. However, there are times when we all have to step back and sometimes that is a very wise thing to do but we can always pray.

In that place

It may be that you are the person heading in a direction you never thought you'd be taking. Things seem to be going wrong for you and you wish it was all over, or you are close to someone who is causing you great distress. I have met a few women who have asked what the point of going on was. They appeared to be in such a 'dark' place with little hope. There may be some things going on that you just don't understand and where you are right now may appear very lonely and scary. Many of the women and family members find great comfort in the Footprints poem, where two sets of footprints become one – at this point it is because one person is being carried and not abandoned.

I really believe that at our lowest point God will send support. It may be in the form of an angel or a friend or a professional. It may be that God will open a 'door' or cause something unexpected to happen. Sometimes we don't recognise it as God's hand at work. I'm happy to call these 'God incidents'. It is almost as if something miraculous takes place which is beyond explanation. Take time to reflect and seek wisdom. That offer of support may be God-sent.

I am convinced that there will be many people who have been in dark places, consumed by addiction, having suffered horrendous life journeys, who will hear God's words 'Well done good and faithful servant' when they enter eternity. Those are the words of Jesus as found in Matthew 25:23 and refer to the parable of the bags of gold. In Jesus' parable the master was pleased with the way some of his servants had managed the gold given them and gave it back having invested it well, with a return of a little more than when they received it. I believe God is pleased with those who, whilst have had little, have used what they had well. Some people have held on to their belief and trust in God even though they have gone through dark valleys. The faith they had, however fragile, they have held on to and in many cases have increased it. I have prayed with many women who say their faith is even stronger than before they went into prison. The journey may not define you but how you respond to it may. I referred to this scripture in the Introduction and it is appropriate to use it towards the end of the book: 'And surely I am with you always, to the very end of the age' (Matthew 28:20).

Walking through

Who knows where life's journey may take us. When I joined the Army, which, as you know, turned about to be for only a few months, I never thought I'd work in a prison or become a chaplain, especially after the frank words of the padre. By the time this book is published I will have been walking women from the prison to the train station on a regular basis for over twenty-four months. When I stepped down from being Managing Chaplain of the prison I didn't know then that I would become a through-the-gate chaplaincy expert and write this book or even get it published. But I'm a believer in stepping out of comfort zones and seeing doors open that appear to have heavy bolts and the words KEEP OUT on them. But when God unlocks the door and opens it, then surely it is one's duty to walk through it. So I'm 'walking' and I'll stop when it's time to stop. God may at some point make it very clear he wants me to do something else and my season of journeying to the station may end. But for now it's 'keep going' and that's my message to everyone who wants to give up now – 'keep going'.

Resilience

I am amazed at the resilience some women show, especially those who are caught in the cycle of vulnerability, addiction, criminality and imprisonment, then to be released with no fixed abode and vulnerable. They keep on keeping on. Some reflect upon their 'lot' in life and accept 'it is what it is'. Others are focused on a brighter future which must surely come one day – or so they hope. What lies ahead can be challenging whoever we are, and we all have a story to tell of overcoming difficulties. Some readers may say that they have never experienced the criminal justice system or even know anyone who has. Some may say that they have never had to overcome a disability, however minor like mine. But many will have faced confusion, frustration and pain – just like the two walking on the road to Emmaus. I have been writing this book for several months and over that period I have come across a few 'ups' and 'downs'. When travelling through the downs I have imagined Jesus walking alongside me and pre-empting what he might say to my confusion or frustration. This has sometimes brought a little smile to my face as I have visualised him listening to my woes and then saying, 'Come on, Simeon, you didn't know this was going to happen, but you know the answer.' Then after a short reflection I end up giving myself the advice I'm sure he would give if he were standing next to me in person. Just recently I tried to organise a local event. Someone sent me an email concerning it which frustrated me for a short while. I reflected upon what Jesus would have said, dusted myself down, replied in a positive manner and carried on with the journey – going back to the state of mind I should be in. Sometimes the journey is an emotional one, not just physical. Sometimes we need to get back emotionally to the 'right' place, the healthy place, walking through the difficulties until we find ourselves back where we know we should be.

Mary

The other day Mary, a newer volunteer, assisted me as we journeyed to the station with two women. Mary was in the Community Coffee Shop when we turned up and, after a hot drink each, we set off down the road. We weren't in a particular hurry to start the trip as it was raining heavily, but in the end we had to brave it. We all popped into the off-licence to keep out of the rain. One of the women bought two cans of beer, the other one bought lots of sweets. The rain continued to pour down but we had to step out into it in order not to miss the next train and wait half an hour. We got to the station on time, changed the travel warrants and waved the women off on their train. As they got on they thanked us for coming out in the rain to escort them.

We had spent about forty minutes with them, had no specific 'life-changing' conversation or done anything they couldn't have done without us. I could see Mary was a little deflated, and as it was still raining heavily I suggested we went for a coffee near the station to mull over what had taken place and keep dry. She was a bit disappointed and obviously felt we had achieved very little. It was almost as if this time she didn't have much to share with anyone, as previously she had gone back to her family and shared how she'd listened to someone's worries, whilst of course not disclosing any confidentialities. This time all she'd done was to carry a redundant crutch for one of the women – hardly headline news and nothing special.

Over coffee I went through what had just taken place and the significant impact we had just made. The women knew Mary was a volunteer who had come quite a distance. I highlighted that her huge effort for no monetary reward, putting herself out to walk in the rain had not been 'lost' on the women, as indicated by their thanks as they embarked upon the next stage of their journey. I noted that the women hadn't opened the cans of alcohol and had got on the train sober and in good time for their appointments. I also noted that when they left they were smiling and grateful. I underlined the fact that they had the best start to the day because we journeyed with them and that they would have felt 'special', special enough for us to put ourselves out for them. That simple 'no frills' walk in the rain was one of great value and not to be underestimated.

Nothing special

It is easy to think that we have done nothing special. Yet what one person regards as ordinary another perceives as lovely. I have a friend who does 'lovely' regularly without even knowing it. Kaz has a 'foothills' ministry, as I call it. She has a physical disability which limits her mobility but doesn't stop her ministry. She once dreamt of going to China as a missionary but getting from London to Brighton is now a major mission. However, Kaz loves talking to people, whoever they are. She'll chat in a queue, listen to someone on a bus and offer tender encouragement in a coffee shop; nothing high profile or worthy of flag waving but hugely important to the lonely and isolated who may not have spoken to anyone that day until she came along. It may not be mountain-peak ministry but it is vital for those struggling half way up or down. I know Kaz doesn't think her ministry is particularly special but for the person who engages with her it can change their ordinary day into a special one.

Simple acts of kindness can have a profound effect. Walking alongside a lonely, scared and disorientated person can leave them feeling valued and respected. The women I walk with are all

God's creation, each one unique and special to him. What does it cost to smile at someone or ask how they are? One day I may be in need of a smile and a greeting, I may be lost or lonely, in need of a helping hand and a word of encouragement. One day I may need you.

Reflection

Luke 24:32-33

They asked each other, 'Were not our hearts burning within us while he talked with us on the road and opened the Scriptures to us?' They got up and returned at once to Jerusalem.

Full of passion

It is fitting to finish with this passage again as it inspires me every time I read it. I opened the book with it and reflected upon it in chapter 6. After the two had encountered Jesus they responded passionately. I like to think they dropped everything and got back to the others as soon as they possibly could. They knew what they should do and they did it. The encounter was life changing. However, I don't doubt that there are some of us who would question whether we would have gone back straight away. Some of us may have thought we better sleep on things and then go back in the morning. Others of us may 'self-talk' ourselves out of taking any action. Then again, some of us may be inclined to encourage the other one to go back and we'd follow later. Some might say that until we are in the same position the Emmaus two were in, we wouldn't really know how we would respond. Some people who have read this book, engaged with the journey of the Emmaus road travellers and pondered the anecdotal stories of those women I have walked to the station, may not know how to respond, and that is OK. It may take a while to process what you've read and reflect upon the issues and opportunities.

If you do nothing else can I please ask you to pray once for the people who have left prison today? If you can, perhaps you may remember them in prayer weekly or monthly? However, it may be that as you have read about the various journeys in the book and gone on to answer the questions, you have come to see how much in common you may have with those leaving prison. Not that you specifically relate to the physical journey of coming out of prison but that you may identify with some of the emotions and thoughts that many experience. If this is the case then perhaps God is calling you or your church to get more involved. Maybe God is turning your compassion into passion and your empathy into action.

Questions

1. Have your thoughts changed or been challenged regarding people who have been in prison?
2. Having read the book, what one thing has most challenged you specifically regarding the situation facing women as they leave prison?
3. Can you think of anything that you have been challenged over regarding your own life's journey?
4. Having seen the way Jesus journeyed with the two on the road to Emmaus, would you now be able to walk with people walking in the 'wrong direction'?

For prayer

Please pray for wisdom and guidance in how to respond to what you have read. Please pray for those people leaving prison without anywhere safe to stay and pray for resources to be made available in order to meet the various needs of those re-joining society.

Acknowledgements

An enormous thank you goes out to so many people. Unfortunately I cannot mention you all by name but I am grateful to everyone who has journeyed with me. In fact I was going to remove everyone's name and replace it with a number, similar to the numbers prisoners receive upon entry into the prison system. I decided against that but have chosen to mention everyone by first name only, keeping some anonymity for those who would prefer it that way.

I will start, however, by thanking the women, for allowing me to journey with them at what can be a particularly vulnerable time for them as they step back into the world and begin to face the various challenges that lie before them.

Thanks also go to the local community who have embraced what I do and in so many ways 'stand' or 'walk' beside me and the women who journey through their community. Thank you to Paul and Gillian, Aimee, Jean and Sue, and all those at the local Salvation Army. Thanks also go to Fr Joseph and the local Anglican church and to all those who volunteer, especially Beryl, Avis, Cherie, Maria, Ruthie, Cath and Joanna.

A huge thank you to Pastor Desmond and my church family for all your encouragement, enthusiasm and prayer support.

To Chris, Gary, Graham, Sharon, Marian, Linda, Leon, Terry, Andy, Paul, Caroline, Barry, Samantha, Nigel, Dorota, Bally and all those who have assisted with the manuscript – read it, made useful suggestions and listened to me as I've wrestled with the ministry and book project – I thank you. I'm also extremely grateful to the encouragement I have received from Pastor Fred and the Revd Canon Selwyn in Ghana; and Ioana and John in Romania. A special thank you is given to Fiona for writing the foreword – what a journey you have been on; I'm so proud to call you a friend.

To Malcolm and Sarah who have given me the steer and their wisdom, enabling the project to come to fruition.

To my chaplaincy work colleagues past and present, especially Carol and Marcel. For those who have employed me, endorsed me and given me the opportunities to engage in this ministry.

To my wonderful family – Julie, Kat, Andy, Dan and Ruairi, Dad and Carole, and Mum (in-law) – a very special thank you for all your love, patience and support. And to God for making me who I am and loving me as you do.

Simeon

If you want to contact Simeon please email:
s-sturney@hotmail.com